Redefining the Top 1%

PRAISE FOR *REDEFINING THE TOP 1%*

"The best leaders are deeply driven to help improve the lives of others. *Redefining The Top 1%* inspires and equips each of us to be better leaders and better humans, while guiding those around us onto the same path."

> -**Marshall Goldsmith**, Thinkers 50 #1 Executive Coach
> and only two-time #1 Leadership Thinker in the world
> #1 *New York Times* Best Selling Author of *Triggers*

"When you think about reaching the Top 1%, what comes to mind? In *Redefining The Top 1%*, Blattner challenges the traditional notion of powerful leadership by making it very personal, and very attainable."

> -**Sydney Finkelstein**, Director of the Center for Leadership at
> the Tuck School of Business at Dartmouth College,
> Bestselling Author of *Superbosses*

"*Redefining the Top 1%* is a powerful and instructive book for growth-minded leaders. Trevor Blattner's compelling, research-based model for Shepherd Leadership contains practical tools and clear steps to transcend the ordinary and achieve like those in the Top 1%. If you lead, aspire to lead, or seek extraordinary results in just about any endeavor, read this book."

> -**Mark E. Green**, Author of *Activators - A CEO's Guide to
> Clearer Thinking and Getting Things Done* and
> *Creating a Culture of Accountability*, speaker, business
> and leadership growth coach to CEOs and executive teams

"'Imagine if you could redefine yourself to be anyone you want to be.' To me, these words capture the essence of Dr. Trevor Blattner's new book *Redefining The Top 1%*. If you've been through times when you have asked yourself, 'What's the point of it all?' - you have to read this book. It's not cheerleading. It's not empty 'feel good' platitudes. This is a guidebook to changing your life in ways that can lead to fulfillment at every level. Highest recommendation."

-**Joe Calloway**, Bestselling Author of
Becoming a Category of One

"ATTACKING the 1% mindset isn't for everyone. Is it for YOU? Trevor unpacks what it takes, how to think and how YOUR next level is YOUR choice. Don't hold back. Embrace the opportunity to grow with Trevor in this tactical guide to YOUR 1%."

-**Ben Newman**, Globally Recognized Performance Coach

"If you're ready to take full responsibility for your life and share your talents with the world, this book will give you the inspiration and motivation you need."

-**Dorie Clark**, author of *Reinventing You* and
Entrepreneurial You, and executive education faculty,
Duke University Fuqua School of Business

"A must-read for anyone involved in the art of authentic Influence. This book is about making a significant difference in the world by leading from the inside out. The system of behaviors Trevor teaches are meant to transform you both personally and professionally. Read this, and then go lead with integrity."

-**Chris Widener**, author of *Lasting Impact: Creating a Life*
and *Business that Lives Beyond You*

"The step-by-step system of behaviors Blattner outlines in *Redefining The Top 1%* makes the often daunting idea of effective leadership both concrete and achievable."

-**Dr. Tasha Eurich**, New York Times Bestselling Author of *Insight* and *Bankable Leadership*.

"A must-read book for change-agents! *Redefining The Top 1%* takes an action-oriented approach to developing authentic influence from the inside out. If you want to make a significant difference in the world, and become the leader others want to follow, Trevor's book is your guide."

-**Teresa de Grosbois**, International Bestselling Author of *Mass Influence*

"Regardless of your age or experience, *REDEFINING THE TOP 1%* will shift your perspective on what it takes to reach greatness in your personal life and in your ability to lead others."

-**Joel Brown**, Founder of Addicted2Success

"Somewhere in the nexus of responsibility, generosity and commitment we're able to find the ability to do work that matters. This book can open the door to that path."

-**Seth Godin**, Bestselling Author of *The Practice*

"Great leaders build great teams on the foundation of excellence. Excellence starts with inspirational leadership. This book provides you with a blueprint to inspire your team and build your culture to take your organization to the next level."

-**Anton Gunn**, Former Senior Advisor to President Barack Obama and the world's leading authority on Socially Conscious Leadership.

"I firmly believe that each of us has been created with a unique purpose and passion, and with all the resources needed already within us to live it out. Success in life is NEVER based on luck, and the key behaviors that Trevor lays out in *Redefining The Top 1%* gives you a remarkable set of tools to tap into these resources and create your own 'luck.'"

-**Paul Martinelli**, Success Coach and President
of The John Maxwell Team

REDEFINING THE TOP 1%

——7 Behaviors——
That Drive
Shepherd Leadership

DR. TREVOR BLATTNER

NEW YORK

LONDON • NASHVILLE • MELBOURNE • VANCOUVER

Redefining the Top 1%

7 Behaviors that Drive Shepherd Leadership

© 2021 Dr. Trevor Blattner

Published in New York, New York, by Morgan James Publishing. Morgan James is a trademark of Morgan James, LLC. www.MorganJamesPublishing.com

Morgan James BOGO™

A **FREE** ebook edition is available for you or a friend with the purchase of this print book.

CLEARLY SIGN YOUR NAME ABOVE

Instructions to claim your free ebook edition:
1. Visit MorganJamesBOGO.com
2. Sign your name CLEARLY in the space above
3. Complete the form and submit a photo of this entire page
4. You or your friend can download the ebook to your preferred device

ISBN 9781631953262 paperback
ISBN 9781631953330 eBook
Library of Congress Control Number:
2020918381

Cover Design by:
Kelly Mariko Nishimura

Interior Design by:
Christopher Kirk
www.GFSstudio.com

Morgan James is a proud partner of Habitat for Humanity Peninsula and Greater Williamsburg. Partners in building since 2006.

Get involved today! Visit
MorganJamesPublishing.com/giving-back

This book is dedicated to all those who believe that leading, growing and optimizing elite businesses is the most efficient way to make a major contribution to the human condition and to the lights of my life, Ashley, Kate, Nora, and Lenna.

CONTENTS

ACKNOWLEDGMENTS

There are many people to thank who were part of my journey in writing this book.

To my wonderful wife, Ashley, and our three amazing girls, Kate, Nora, and Lenna. I know the timing was anything but ideal when I officially decided to undertake the project of writing this book. The patience, faith, and support you have shown me (even in moments when you were forced to fake it) has made all the difference. You and our girls inspire me to be a better man each and every day. I love you.

To my parents, Rick and Tracy Blattner, who gave me the independence and trust I needed from a very early age to pursue my own path and learn from my mistakes. We don't get to choose the family we're born into, but I thank God every day for both of you.

To my entire team at BEC. Tori, Joy, Denise, Kelcie, and Jess: You have each endured my intensity and singleness of focus for the last year with extreme grace and understanding. I'm blessed to have each of you in my life.

To my editor, Justin Spizman, who has been a valued resource and a joy to work with on the project.

To Terry, Gayle, David, and the entire team at Morgan James Publishing, for all of their support and hard work in bringing this book to life.

To Matt McWilliams, Bryan Wish, Carson Morell, Rich Keller, and Mark Green for going above and beyond supporting me in getting these ideas into the world.

And to you, the reader. Thank you for taking the time to read my work. I pray it has been of value to you.

INTRODUCTION

A s the world turns, so does the human performance bar. It certainly seems to be at an all-time high as I write this book. No matter how you perceive it, there is a great deal of pressure to perform at high levels. That pressure then turns into negative responses. Data shows that the use of antidepressants by Americans rose 400% from 1988 to 2008, and anxiety is at an all-time high as well.[1] Between 1999 and 2014 there was a 64% increase in the use of antidepressants as well. All of this has only been amplified by the COVID-19 Pandemic.[2] It is fair to say that this is likely a result of the increased weight of the world on our shoulders.

---

1   Antidepressant Use in Persons Aged 12 and Over: United States, 2005–2008, National Center for Health Statistics, October 2011, available online at https://www.cdc.gov/nchs/products/databriefs/db76.htm.

2   Ettman CK, Abdalla SM, Cohen GH, Sampson L, Vivier PM, Galea S. Prevalence of Depression Symptoms in US Adults Before and During the COVID-19 Pandemic. *JAMA Netw Open.* 2020;3(9):e2019686. doi:10.1001/jamanetworkopen.2020.19686

As Gallup CEO Jim Clifton points out, "an increasing number of people in the world are miserable, hopeless, suffering, and becoming dangerously unhappy...."[3] To build on this point, a recent article in the *New York Post* by Rich Lowry states: "The decline [in life expectancy] isn't hitting older Americans, who are still making improvements, but is cutting down people in the prime of their lives, ages 25-64. The odds that a 32-year-old will die in a given year rose by almost 25 percent between 2012-14 and 2015-17. American adulthood has suddenly become more lethal than it has been in decades.... To put it bluntly, contemporary America is characterized by less procreation and more self-destruction. This suggests that something is profoundly wrong with the state of the union, although it doesn't receive the attention and the debate it deserves."[4] Scary, right?

In reality it all starts at the individual level. We not only have to put people first, but we have to collectively work together to embrace our shortcomings and improve them. As each of us fights hard to develop and evolve, we all win. If we are to fix this broken version of our society, it must be from the ground level up. If you've picked up this book, you likely fall into one of three categories of people:

1. Your world is crumbling and collapsing underneath your feet. You feel like there's nowhere else to go and you're about to bail out of life completely. If this is you, you're not alone. This book and the philosophy of living it espouses will give you a renewed sense of life.

2. You are the person everyone says is doing "great." Everything in life is fine; you've gotten very good at painting the plastered smile on your face and offering the fake handshake.

---

3   Clifton, Jim. *The Coming Jobs War*, 2011, Washington DC: Gallup Press, pp. 1-2.

4   Lowry, Rich. Falling births and rising deaths: two signs of an unseen American crisis, *New York Post*, December 4, 2019, available online at https://nypost.com/2019/12/04/falling-births-and-rising-deaths-two-signs-of-an-unseen-american-crisis.

Meanwhile, *your soul is empty* and *your internal world is miserable*. Read on.

3. You are doing so well that you've reached a place of complete boredom and stagnation. And you've got that nasty feeling in your gut that asks, *Is this really all there is? Is this it?* Well, NO. It's not. Just stay with me.

The most fundamental duty of a leader is to navigate both themselves and others through tumultuous and uncertain times. The pandemic and subsequent social upheaval have revealed a troubling divide in our country. This raises a question: How did we get here?

Our leaders turned a blind eye. The people we put in power—those who are supposed to guide us—have let inequity build below the surface. Now we're seeing the effects. If we want to build a better world, we must prioritize people over everything else, including money, power, and status. If we want to emerge from this better than before, *we have to rethink leadership*.

My core thesis throughout our time together will be that you must break away from the current trend of despair and self-destruction by becoming a leader of yourself and those around you. And not just any sort of leader, but a very particular type of leader. You must become a *Shepherd Leader*. In doing so you will find a valuable release and open the doors to growth and a sense of peace in your life.

It is not an accident to reach the top 1% in your field in terms of wealth and influence. To do so, you must learn the systematic process of how to behave, think, and perform like similarly situated people. Anyone can achieve it—especially someone like you—if you're willing to follow the step-by-step behaviors and actions laid out for you in this book. The Top 1% System and Shepherd Leadership are not about appearing to be hardcore and arrogant. Rather, they are centered on performing at your absolute maximum capacity. That goes for whether you are a parent, a small business owner, a student, or the CEO of a major corporation.

What you'll find throughout the behaviors taught in this book is that we all face similar battles. There is only one enemy you must defeat as you adopt the Top 1% philosophy to become a high-performing Shepherd Leader. You are intimately familiar with this enemy. This enemy is YOU. It is infinitely simple yet overwhelmingly difficult to compete against yourself. Imagine if you could redefine yourself to be anyone you want to be. The possibilities are limitless. Nothing in your life is permanent; it's all progressing based on your choices, behaviors, and actions.

The ultimate success marker is how much good you do for others. This is the reason I want you to be successful. The more wealth you produce, the more good you can do for others and the more wealth you can help *them* produce.

Redefining the Top 1% is about personal transformation, transcending perceived limitations, and ultimately reaching extreme success and generosity. This is a system—or philosophy, if you like—backed by scientific evidence that supports each of the behaviors outlined herein.

If you take only one thing away from our time together, my sincerest wish is that you would take full responsibility for your own life. You're not the one getting the check every two weeks, you're the one writing the checks. You've made the decision to shoulder the burden, in exchange for the autonomy and unlimited potential for growth. For that I salute you. You are already a hero. But you can't stop there and remain complacent. You must keep growing and serving. You've been called to a higher responsibility.

Servant Leadership is not about being the best just so you can beat everyone else, though that will be a natural byproduct of adopting these behaviors. It's about being the best you can possibly be so that you can bring the highest level of impact and generosity to the world at large and, perhaps more importantly, to those you're in immediate contact with.

I want you to be able to give more energy and financial resources to those people who rely on you so that they can pay their bills and provide for their families because of the salary and bonuses you give them. I want you to be able to give more to organizations you care about, like your local church, or mission work, or the homeless, or whatever particular organization has had an impact on your life. I want you to be able to provide for your own family in a way that you never dreamed possible before. I also think it's vitally important that you model for those around you, including your kids, what life can be like when you adopt these behaviors as your life philosophy.

I hope, whatever you believe, you do so with vigor, passion, and intensity. I hope it radiates from you in a way that shows through in everything you do in your life, because that is how life is meant to be lived. Current and aspiring business leaders and entrepreneurs are the group of people that make the world go round. You stay up late, you get up early, you're responsible for the livelihood of everyone on your team, and you have a mission. You are my hero. It's time to be bold about who you really are and what you really stand for. You've earned it, your team will admire you for it, and the world desperately needs you to do it. The world needs you to be a Shepherd Leader.

The Top 1% philosophy is based not just on a set of "success" principles, but on a series of steps that serve to build deep and profound *character* into your life and behavior. Character determines who you are. Who you are becomes a foundation for everything you do. Your character is foundational to your effectiveness as a Shepherd Leader and Top 1% performer. As Emerson said, "What you are shouts so loudly in my ears, I cannot hear what you say."

A great conflict results when the things you do from moment to moment are disconnected from your being, the essence of who you are at the core. One of the great secrets of success and achievement is to constantly connect your *doing* and your *being* from moment to moment. In other words, in everything you do, do it with all your heart and soul and mind, and do it in a way that is uniquely your style and highlights your gifts and the infinite power you were gifted with. Don't be somewhere else in your mind. Don't be halfhearted in anything you do.

We are each battling demons. Real demons. Symptoms of this include the symptoms of Alpha 1.0, the tendency toward ego-driven, self-focused, scarcity-oriented thinking and behavior. It's marked by a need to hide insecurity by acquiring power and authority, though in some circumstances they may go even beyond those. The point is that these demons must be dealt with and destroyed. You and I have the free will to *choose* to destroy those demons. And we must destroy them if we hope to reach the Top 1%. I know you want that, you deserve that, and I desperately want that for you.

Escape is not the answer; neither is addiction. You cannot escape yourself, at the end of the day and at the end of your life. The person you fundamentally are is always in full view to you. This book will require you to dig deep for answers not out in the world somewhere, but inside yourself. There is no answer out there—you and your personal transformation are the answer. Study these behaviors and integrate them with discipline into your life, and you will transform yourself into a Shepherd Leader.

Let me put this another way: you must succeed, and you must win. We need you to reach the Top 1%. We need you to be a Shepherd Leader.

Chapter 1

THE TOP 1%—AN OVERVIEW

You and I, and the other 99% of the world, have been living our lives as disciples of a philosophy called Alpha 1.0. Like the other 99%, you suffer from insecurity, indecision, inauthenticity, limitation, and, in most cases, desperation. You're not satisfied and fulfilled in the life you're living, and you never will be if you continue to buy into the Alpha 1.0 paradigm. You wake in the morning with a feeling in your soul that you are not living up to your true potential. You're restless, you're bored, and you might be a little scared. You're probably angry too, though you may not admit it.

Your days are likely bursting at the seams with activities and events, and yet simultaneously they are quietly desperate and empty. Your most valuable relationships are stagnant, and your other relationships remain superficial because you feel the constant need to impress others so they will perceive you as worthy of their admiration. You desire to reach the top of your profession and increase your overall contribution, but you don't think it's possible for you. You know there is a unique mission, a calling even, for you to accomplish, but you just can't get yourself to pursue it with all your heart. Forcing this calling to go away creates pain. To escape the pain, you turn to distraction (i.e., alcohol, smoking, social media, television, pornography, or whatever it is in your life). Alpha 1.0 owns you.

I know this because a decade of my life was defined by my own anxiety, insecurity, self-doubt, and even self-hate. I had this sense of inner chaos and turmoil that I just wasn't equipped to handle. I sabotaged several relationships, I suddenly got sick more often, and I relied on alcohol far too often to ease the pain. The final straw for me came when a physician diagnosed me with generalized anxiety disorder. I felt imprisoned by this condition. To quote Steven Pressfield, "The pain of being human is that we're all angels imprisoned in vessels of flesh."[5] This diagnosis forced me to make a major decision in my life. I could become a victim and use the anxiety as an excuse for mediocrity, or I could figure out a way to transcend the anxiety and use it to my advantage.

I had studied personal development and success since I first read Napoleon Hill's[6] *Think and Grow Rich* at the age of nineteen. But it took me about ten years of continuous study in multiple fields before the lightbulb really came on. Once I got a clear understanding of the interconnectedness of all the different branches of science, along with the Laws of Achievement, everything clicked, and life has never been the same. Since that time, my goal has been to create a reproducible system to guide others.

---

5   Pressfield, Steven. *Turning Pro: Tap Your Inner Power and Create Your Life's Work*, New York: Black Irish Entertainment LLC, 2012.

6   Hill, Napoleon. *Think and Grow Rich*, New York: Ballantine Books, 1983 (note there are many editions of this classic that first appeared in 1937, some abridged and others unabridged).

You must become a disciple of the Shepherd Leadership philosophy to be part of the Top 1%. As a Shepherd Leader you will find your self-respect again and tap into a dormant power you never knew you had. You will begin to feel your calling and pursue it with everything you have. No one is born a Shepherd Leader, but if you wish to grow into full maturity as the best version of your possible self, you must become one before it's too late.

The Four Levels of Personal Performance

As a practicing endodontist who runs a busy office, and as a personal performance coach to fellow business leaders, I spend a lot of time studying the fields of neuroscience, quantum physics, performance psychology, success, and leadership. I'm continuously learning and integrating information to enhance my own knowledge and improve the lives of others.

Over the last several years, I've been privileged to mentor others through the process of implementing what I call Optimized Performance Protocols (OPPs). Throughout my study and interaction with my students, I've gradually put together a framework called the Four Levels of Personal Performance. Throughout these pages I will break down each of the four levels so you can understand a bit more about the way life works and where we get stuck as human beings. I'll be referring to these four levels on our journey together.

The first level is *Mayhem*. At this base level you're really in survival mode where you're putting out fires, searching for immediate gratification, and just trying to get through the day with as little pain as possible. Unfortunately, for many people this is the normal default level of performance. It's not only unsatisfying, it's also deeply unhealthy both emotionally and physically. We'll get deeper into the science on this, but for now just understand that at the level of Mayhem, your immune system suffers, your ability to think clearly is impaired, and you're in no frame of mind to do meaningful work in the world.

Level two is *Mediocrity*. This is where the majority of people stay for most of their lives. The challenge with Mediocrity is that an infinite number of other people are at this level of performance, and *very little pain* is associated with it. The pain that is associated with it is often soothed by well-meaning others who tell you it's "okay" to keep doing what you're doing and that you're doing "the best you can." To me it's very clear this is what Thoreau was referring to when he said "the mass of men lead lives of quiet desperation."[7] One thing to note that's a bit counterintuitive is how there's *so much less competition at the top*. Mediocrity and Mayhem are the areas where almost everyone stays and where all the competition fights for positioning, but at the top, in the Top 1%, competition is not an issue. This is why you must move beyond level two as quickly as possible.

Level three is *Mission*. I'll be honest: Getting to level three takes an immense amount of commitment, focus, and discipline because you've transcended the level of Mediocrity and you've got a pretty clear set of goals and purpose to which you're aiming. At the Mission level, you are choosing your actions to align with your overall life vision with intent. In fact, in many cases you've already set up systems and delegated some things, so you're able to do more and perform better than the majority of people in the world.

A major shift, though, takes place between level three and level four, the highest level, which I refer to as *Mastery*.

Mastery is the level of personal performance where everything you do happens predictably and fluidly, with very little friction and maximum joy and self-expression. When you reach the level of Mastery, you have a deep understanding of an optimized environment, how to care for

---

7   The quote can be found in the first chapter of Henry David Thoreau's classic book, *Walden*.

and control your mind (your most powerful tool), and how to get into the state of flow or "in the zone" daily, where you're firing on all cylinders, free from resistance. Mastery is the ultimate level and the level to which I know you aim—and the level I'm going to help you reach.

The Shepherd Leadership Philosophy

To work through these four levels, we now turn to the Shepherd Leadership philosophy, which is a set of behaviors that are ideally cultivated in sequential order. As you can see in the diagram below, as you perfect each behavior you move through the ladder from a state of Mayhem toward Mastery.

For example, you should perfect behaviors one and two before you can effectively adopt behaviors three and four. And it is crucial to find solidity in behaviors three and four before jumping to behaviors five and six. Behavior number seven is unique because it is spiritual in nature and designed to permeate each of the other six behaviors, tying them together and creating synergy between them to make each one more effective. It is a natural accelerator of sorts. Now this does not mean that you must perfect each behavior before working on the next. I don't advocate putting your life on hold as you try to reach perfection. But you'll find that the behaviors I've laid out for you are most advantageous if developed in sequence. Take a look at the following model *(on next page)* that outlines your forthcoming journey.

The first two behaviors, outlined in the following chapters, focus on shifting from a state of chaos called Mayhem to the second level of personal performance, known as Mediocrity. These are the initial steps along the path to personal excellence. Behaviors three and four take you to a very high level of performance and leadership, namely into a defined Mission. And behaviors five and six are indicative of movement toward a Mastery level of leadership and performance. But

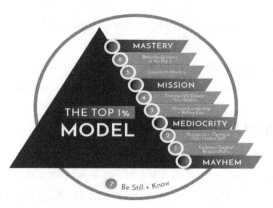

the true hallmark of Mastery is the spiritual component, which brings everything together in behavior number seven.

Each consecutive step transcends and includes the one prior to it. Einstein said, "You can't solve a problem on the same level of consciousness where the problem was created." Every consecutive step along the ladder raises your level of awareness and consciousness regarding what's possible and what's most effective. Each behavior builds on the one before it. You must literally think at a higher level and understand success, as well as the processes and universal laws that go along with it. Eben Pagan, one of my favorite teachers, talks about the idea that success is an emergent.[8] In other words, it's not a cause-and-effect relationship but rather the result of the seven behaviors I'm going to teach you all working together in concert, allowing success to emerge on a higher level.

So how do you now take this awareness of the Four Levels of Personal Performance and apply the steps in a way that will supercharge your own personal achievement? The answer lies in the Seven Key Behaviors of the Shepherd Leader. Putting ideas into motion is the most important thing about any training program, including this one. Doing the exercises and allowing your mind to be transformed by them is the most important piece in the learning process.

---

8   See Eben Pagan's website at https://ebenpagantraining.com/about.

I call these principles *behaviors* because that's exactly what they are. The Shepherd Leadership System is a way of behaving on a daily basis, and since these are the behaviors of the super successful, adopting them in sequential order makes success inevitable. The major caveat here, of course, is that it requires the *decision* to become successful and to put these behaviors into practice day in and day out to guarantee success. The decision is the critical moment. *Go ahead and make that decision right now.*

We are facing a challenging time in history. As uncertainty and stress continue to rise, so does the fear of the future. Everyone is asking themselves, "What happens next?" No one can really say for sure. But one thing I do know is this: *We need leaders.* Not only are leaders needed right now, but I will go as far as to say they are *essential.* Why? Leaders inspire. They use their perspective, influence, and passion to guide others through tough times.

And right now we need them more than ever.

Let's get started!

EXERCISE: Imprinting Revealed

This exercise is designed to expose any flawed subconscious thought patterns you have. You can then begin the process of changing those beliefs to ones that better serve you.

We all wanted love or affection as a child. As we grew, we complicated things by creating a set of guidelines based on what type of person we "needed to be" to receive that love or affection. We refer to these guidelines as imprints. The problem is that many times people will spend their entire lives living by the imprinting they created subconsciously as a child, even if it is no longer beneficial to them as an adult.

To that end, the following questions will help you become aware of some of your existing imprints that you might need to alter:

1. As a child, who did you want love from the most? This is usually not who you got it from but instead the person you wanted love from the most. (examples: mom, dad, grandparents, etc.)

2. What type of person did you believe you "had to be" to receive that person's love? (examples: smart, funny, creative, strong, self-sufficient, an achiever, etc.)

3. What type of person did you believe you could never be? (if you were this type of person, they would immediately take away their love)

4. Who are you today?

5. Who would you need to become (by adding or taking away some traits or actions) to be the type of man or woman who would easily achieve all the goals you are aiming for in life? (And enjoy the process as well)

Keep the answers to this exercise close by as we will reference them again later in the book. For now, this should help you gain a greater sense of awareness of the subconscious thinking that has shaped your behavior—without you ever being consciously aware of it. You can change this thinking if necessary, but you have to recognize it first.

Chapter 2

BEHAVIOR #1:
EMBRACE RADICAL RESPONSIBILITY

The heights by great men reached and kept,
were not attained by sudden flight. But they, while their
companions slept, were toiling upward in the night.
~ Henry Wadsworth Longfellow ~

Through the power of modern science, we are discovering that we have the ability to become exactly who we desire to be. Once only supported by philosophy and spirituality, we now can look to scientific evidence for our ability to develop and evolve. But with that power comes great responsibility, requiring enormous decisiveness and action. *It is your responsibility to take control of your life and mind, educate yourself, and learn the things that will allow you to design and build the life you desire.* This singular concept is the foundation of the entire Shepherd Leadership philosophy. It is Behavior #1 in its simplest form. Now let's expand.

We are all born with a set of these gifts internally wired within us that serve as our potential. Even so, it's up to us as individuals to hone and sharpen our gifts into strengths. We can then align these strengths into opportunities to create value. Your role and responsibilities in this process is to identify your gifts and make the decision to manifest them into strengths and use them productively. *This is one of the great secrets to success.* No one will do this for you—you must make the decision to do it for yourself. This is a strategic process where you're building strengths based on opportunities you can pursue to create maximum value for others.

Noah built the ark. Moses guided his people out of the tyranny of Egypt. George Washington fathered a nation. Martin Luther King Jr. put his dream of a world where one is not judged by skin color but by the content of their character above his own safety. Abraham Lincoln led the nation at a time of great divide to emancipate slaves. David slayed Goliath. Rocky avenged Apollo by beating down Ivan Drago. And Jesus Christ was willingly tortured and crucified for the sins of all mankind.

Each of the above examples is the result of a human individual deciding to draw a line in the sand and take full ownership of the situation without excuse (okay, Jesus falls into a category of one). Your potential is limitless, but potential is really nothing more than disordered and unchanneled energy. To embrace radical responsibility is to demand of yourself that the unfocused potential energy at your disposal be put into order by your moment-to-moment decision making.

The greatest leaders in their respective fields of leadership and success embrace what I call *radical responsibility*, where they accept no excuses from themselves or others. They simply make the decision to use the resources they have to find solutions to the problems they must overcome. This is the behavior you're going to develop now. This is a non-negotiable behavior if you are striving to reach the Top 1%. And for our purposes, this is the first behavior we will hone on our way to true greatness.

The Shift Occurs Within

To effectuate this goal, you first have to give up the mindset that someone else is going to do this for you. *Nobody else wakes up in the morning with your dreams.* Not. One. Single. Person. Your dreams are all entirely possible, but you must adopt the foundational behavior of embracing radical responsibility before anything else. Realize that you have some crucial role to play in the unfolding of history, and you are therefore morally and ethically obligated to take care of yourself and do your part. Create a compelling vision and go after it every day knowing God made you in His image to bring Him glory through your life and your interaction with others.

The story of a lack of ownership and responsibility is the story of humanity. It goes back as far as human history extends. But it is as insidious and debilitating a problem as ever. It started in the Garden of Eden.

God placed Adam and Eve in the middle of a paradise-like garden. God then commanded Adam and Eve to eat freely from all trees in the garden except *one*, the tree of the knowledge of good and evil. That tree carried the forbidden fruit. It turns out God had very good reasons for advising against eating from this tree (doing so would lead to their death). But God still gave them the ability to *choose* whether to follow His command. As we now know, they disobeyed God's command, and the result was shame and ultimately death. To add insult to injury, Adam blamed both Eve and God for the mistake *he* made

(Genesis 3:12). Not a good start for the dudes out there, right? But you ladies aren't off the hook either. Eve then blamed the Serpent for her actions one verse later. This infamous story is an example of a total lack of ownership.

The key idea here is that there is no freedom without choice. And with no freedom, there is no responsibility. But rest assured God created you to have freedom. And with great freedom comes great responsibility.

Interestingly, the characteristics that make us uniquely human also make us uniquely responsible. Viktor Frankl used the human attribute of self-awareness to point out how between the space of a stimulus and response, only a human being has the free will to make a choice.[9] On top of that, humans have a deep sense of right and wrong that governs our behavior, and an independent will that allows us to take action based on our own self-awareness apart from any other outside influences.

These inherent characteristics bring with them immense responsibility. Your behavior is directly tied to your decisions. You have the freedom and ability to choose your response in each and every scenario. This is a privilege no other creature in the known universe possesses. Don't waste it.

The Root of Your Problems

We have thousands of thoughts every single day. Many of the things you say to yourself are so ruthless they're almost embarrassing to admit. Now, while you may have no say in the automatic reactionary thoughts that come into your mind, you are completely in charge of the significance you attach to each thought.

---

9   The origin of this idea may or may not be attributable to Viktor Frankl, but the point still stands. For a thorough investigation of the idea's origin, see *Quote Investigator* at https://quoteinvestigator.com/2018/02/18/response.

Hopelessness is the root of a great deal of anxiety, depression, and mental illness. It causes addiction and is a source of desperation. Chronic anxiety is based in the fear of not creating the future you desire.

Here are some statistics: in the United States symptoms of depression and anxiety are at an eighty-year high among young people and a twenty-year high in the adult population. Since 1985 men and women have reported lower levels of life satisfaction. Drug overdoses have hit an all-time high as the opioid crisis has hit North America. Nearly half of all Americans report feeling isolated or alone in their lives. And fewer people than ever trust the government, media, or each other. And by the way, these issues are not limited to those with a lower socioeconomic position. In fact, studies are showing that the wealthier you are, and the safer your community, the *more* likely you are to commit suicide![10]

To that end, you likely can conclude that your internal personal problems create many of the problems in your business and relationships. That's right. Your outer circumstances are nothing more than a reflection of your ability to navigate your internal thoughts and challenges. Some gurus refer to this as Inner Game. I just refer to it as Behavior #1.

To embrace radical responsibility means to decide daily, hourly, and moment-to-moment to take the potential given to you by your Creator and make something meaningful and worthwhile out of your brief time on this planet. While it certainly does require sacrifice, the rewards of adopting this behavior are infinite.

One of the fundamental findings of mankind is that when left unattended, the world and everything in it decays and deteriorates. Disorder and chaos are the default settings, not organized order. It's

---

10   Sanburn, Josh. "Why Suicides are More Common in Richer Neighborhoods," *Time Magazine*, November 8, 2012, https://business.time.com/2012/11/08/why-suicides-are-more-common-in-richer-neighborhoods.

only through the practice of embracing radical responsibility that you maintain, create, and improve what would otherwise break down.

To embrace radical responsibility is to accept stewardship of everything entrusted to your care. It is also having the courage to do what you were put on this earth to do. Embrace the calling on your life. You're responsible to provide for, teach, and mentor those in your care as you help them pursue their purpose. Adopt the mindset that you have unique abilities and talents that are marketable and bring enough value to create success for you.

Consequences of Passivity

In 1979, 257 people got on a plane headed for Antarctica from New Zealand. The pilots were unaware that someone had altered the flight coordinates by a seemingly unimportant two degrees. However, this two-degree discrepancy resulted in the plane being 28 miles east of where the pilots planned to be. As they approached Antarctica, the pilots began descending to give the passengers an impressive view of the land. Unfortunately, the incorrect coordinates put them in a direct path with Mount Erebus, an active volcano. It was too late by the time the emergency instruments sounded a warning. The plane crashed into the side of the volcano, killing everyone onboard.

Those seemingly negligible two degrees ended the lives of 257 human beings. In a similar way, all the small things you do, or choose not to do, in life create enormous consequences over time.

The problem with most people is that they're not convinced they must reach the Top 1% level. They haven't chosen a definitive direction. They simply go where life takes them, often resulting in hours of wasted time surfing the internet and making zero progress toward their most sought-after goals. That is an absence of responsibility, a systemic passivity.

Many people think they have to be fully equipped or qualified to take on a particular role or position *before* doing so. That is inaccurate. In fact, it's exactly backwards. After all, how many parents were fully qualified to be excellent caretakers from the day they brought their child home from the hospital? Right, none of you. I wasn't either. You and I became qualified for the role of parenthood by doing it. A trial by fire. Embracing radical responsibility for everything you do is the only requirement of executing the role at a high level. You can't change what you don't take responsibility for. Your past may not be your fault, but your future is your responsibility. The choices of others cannot be controlled, but your choices are your responsibility.

Why Challenge Is Good

In discussing a common characteristic of the affluent in America, Dr. Thomas Stanley remarked: "Courage can be developed. But it cannot be nurtured in an environment that eliminates all risks, all difficulty, all dangers. It takes considerable courage to work in an environment in which one is compensated according to one's performance. What evidence supports this? Most affluent people in America are either business owners or employees who are paid on an incentive basis."[11]

There's a misconception that happiness is the absence of responsibility. We think life should be easy, without challenges and difficulty. But, paradoxically, without a sense of radical responsibility we lack the urgency and commitment and positive pressure to grow and improve. You must have a load to bear and then take responsibility for it to create urgency.

A common example of this, often used by high achievers, is using a financial investment to force you to move forward with a project, idea, or business in order to support this new-founded "expense." I did

11   Stanley, Dr. Thomas and William D. Danko. *The Millionaire Next Door: The Surprising Secrets of America's Wealthy*, Lanham, Maryland: Taylor Trade Publishing, 1996.

this personally when I decided to start my own practice from scratch after residency rather than going into a predictable and high-paying associateship position.

I chose to do this for several reasons, including autonomy and unlimited growth potential. Unfortunately, it would cost me $300,000 (on top of the $200,000 in student debt I had already accrued) to execute the exact type of practice I wanted to create. As you can imagine, this $500,000 chunk of debt served as an immense source of drive and commitment to make my business a success. Knowing that a high investment like this will produce a huge amount of inner commitment, you can use this in your own life to produce serious results. The Top 1% aren't dreamers, they're doers. They're invested, and they take radical responsibility for their investment. You're going to do the same thing.

I hate to break this to you, but if you haven't figured it out yet, life is a continuous series of challenges. And that's okay. You would get stale, bored, and disenchanted if you didn't have problems to challenge you and push you forward to become the type of person who can overcome what needs to be overcome.

Fortunately for you, there are challenges everywhere. Your radical responsibility is to continuously deal with high-level problems rather than low-level problems. Make it your responsibility to deal with problems like how to adjust to incredibly fast business growth rather than problems like how to find enough money to pay all the bills before the month is over. Even people like Bill Gates and Jeff Bezos and Warren Buffett have business and money problems just like everyone else who deals with money and business, but they've taken radical responsibility to rise to a level where their problems are excellent problems to have to deal with and overcome.

You know what Bill Gates and Jeff Bezos and Warren Buffett don't do? They don't blame anyone else for their money and business problems—ever. They embrace radical responsibility for the challenges, and they work with their teams and whoever else they need to bring on board to facilitate solutions to their problems.

Everything in life has an inherent yin-yang property about it. What I mean is that with everything great in life comes the potential for negative. Think about it; the person you love most in the world and choose to spend your life with "till death do us part" is also the person you're most likely to get into a heated argument with. The dream job you now have is also the one that keeps you up at night with stress and anxiety. The leadership position you coveted is now yours, but keeping all the personalities on the team working in the same direction as one cohesive unit is very difficult. This is the yin-yang of life. This is what you signed up for when you got the job, landed the leadership role, and married the man or woman of your dreams. This is where embracing radical responsibility makes all the difference. It's no one else's fault. It's just the nature of life, and you're the only one who has the power to navigate these problems in a beneficial way.

The Motivation Creation Method

Lack of inspiration or motivation, or at least the perception of that lack, is often used as an excuse for a lack of progress in any area of life. But that doesn't have to be the case. There are simple methods you can use to shake yourself out of this perceived mindset and keep rolling forward while embracing radical responsibility. It's called the Motivation Creation Method.

When you feel lack of motivation or inspiration, take immediate action to do something that will move you toward the destination you're seeking. It doesn't really matter what you actually do in your time away. What's important is that you take some particular action to get your mind flowing, get your thoughts moving, and get some feedback. For example, if you're thinking of starting a business but feel overwhelmed, just open a bank account as your first action step. See if that doesn't drive a little bit of inspiration and motivation for you. If you're fighting anxiety or a lack of confidence, admit it to someone or to yourself. That's a very simple action, but it will create inspiration to take the next action. Want to write a book but have no idea how to start? Write two hundred words and see where it takes you.

Pain and suffering in all its various forms is our body's way of pushing us to take action. We will do almost anything to escape pain. In fact, we'll do much more to escape pain and suffering than we will to achieve pleasure and comfort. This is how we're wired. But that's actually not a bad thing. You're lazy sometimes, and so am I. But I'll tell you what…when my life starts to suck and I know it's because of action I haven't taken to make it better, I'm going to take some freaking action to get out of that pain and prevent that future suffering! This is what I mean by radical responsibility.

Are You Willing?

As you're reading this book, completing the exercises, and mapping out exactly the way you want your life to look, ask yourself this question: *What am I willing to take radical responsibility for?*

Several years ago I had the opportunity to hear John C. Maxwell speak. He gave a sermon, and I got to meet him afterwards. It was a cool experience, as he's one of my role models in the field of leadership and spirituality. One thing he said that stuck with me is that he's often asked, "How can I do what you do? How can I become a successful speaker and travel the world like you and become famous?" He said his response is typically, "Well, I know you would love to do what I do, but I'm not sure you'd love to do what I did to become who I am now."

Isn't that true? How many of those people who ask John Maxwell how they can become wealthy and famous and speak on stages all around the world are willing to embrace radical responsibility for putting in the early mornings and late nights writing their keynotes and doing interviews and speaking in rooms with only a few people (instead of five thousand) at the beginning? How many of those people are willing to be laughed at when they tell others what they want to do? Or get turned down the first hundred times they submit a book proposal?

This is what I'm talking about. And the reason I have to start with this foundational behavior is because it paves the way for the remaining six to be more effective. The trap for the 99% is falling in love with *the outcome* without *embracing the process it takes to get there*. The majority fall in love with winning without falling in love with preparation, repetition, training, and practice to become the best before the game ever starts.

I've been heavily influenced by the most successful coaches in athletics. Two who have always separated themselves from the pack in my mind are John Wooden and Mike Krzyzewski. Here is a lesson they both teach: how you run the race, including your planning, preparation, practice, and performance—IS EVERYTHING.

Winning or losing is merely a byproduct of that effort. The quality of your focused effort is what brings the most satisfaction. In fact, before leaving the locker room and entering the arena, whether it was the first game of the season or the national championship game, Coach Wooden's words to his team were always the same: "When it's over, I want your heads up. And there's only one way your heads can be up—that's to give it your very best out there, everything you have."

Compete against yourself. Do the things necessary to call forward your personal best, and don't lose a minute's sleep dwelling on the competition. Let the competition worry about you. You and your team are on a very important mission, and your energy must be focused on what *you* control.

The Cancer You Must Avoid

There is an insidious and somewhat nauseating concept in the world called *entitlement*. Entitlement is like a cancer. It destroys everything it touches. What's worse, it is often asymptomatic to the person who suffers from it because of their own personal delusion about reality. Unfortunately, those who interact with an entitled person often recognize the symptoms all too clearly. They then are affected by them as well. Entitlement is the antithesis of embracing radical responsibility.

To maintain your course and live out your mission requires a sense of control. By control I mean you must feel as though you're in the driver's seat of your own life and able to affect the direction of your life by the actions you take. It is crucial you take this viewpoint from this moment forward.

Victimhood is another word for entitlement. Each of these words elicits a visceral reaction inside me, and they should for you as well. These are both based on a false identity—an identity that needs to prove itself. The one who has been "victimized" in the past therefore "deserves" something as compensation. This is a *loser's philosophy*. You will never accomplish your mission in life or become a Shepherd Leader if you view yourself as a victim in any area of your life or feel entitled to anything simply for being you.

These perspectives on life are nothing more than a disease, and the cure is to embrace radical responsibility in all your life circumstances, as well as your reactions to challenges. The subtle shift from Mediocrity to Mastery is primarily one of posture and attitude, more so than knowledge or skill. Don't many of us still approach life either consciously or subconsciously with the understanding that we are victims of our circumstances?

If you fall into the behavior of talking about how unfair life is, you'll start to fabricate conspiracies in your own mind that do not exist, and studies have shown you'll actually begin putting in less effort at work because you've predetermined it won't accomplish anything. After all, the world is unfair, isn't it? Conversely, if you view success as being just over the horizon, you will not only work diligently to achieve it at higher levels, but you'll also get energy from your work and be more productive. It's a simple change in posture and perspective on the world, but it makes all the difference.

To build and maintain hope in this world, and to deliver hope to others, you must maintain a sense of control over your life and circumstances. By control, I mean you need the sensation that you are captain of the ship and control your ultimate fate. You must have an exciting vision for the future along with the conviction that you're responsible for bringing it into reality. There must be a "something greater" you're pursuing at all times to get the most out of yourself.

This posture toward reality should never be viewed as a burden but rather as an incredible privilege. It's completely within your power to decide how you think about and talk about your problems, both out loud and internally. To quote the great Stoic philosopher Marcus Aurelius, "Reject your sense of injury and your injury itself disappears."

Your Energy Generator

Psychologists use terms like self-determination and autonomy when talking about decisions people make for themselves, based on their own values and purpose. Interestingly, autonomy has been found to be one of the most powerful generators of energy on the planet. Your ability to choose work and projects in line with your mission and purpose will raise your performance and super-charge your energy better than anything else.[12]

12   G.A. Nix, R. M. Ryan, J.B. Manly, and E.L. Deci. Revitalization Through Self-Regulation: The Effects of Autonomous and Controlled Motivation on Happiness and Vitality," *Journal of Experimental Social Psychology* 35, 1999, pp. 266-84.

There's an interesting story about the famous attorney Clarence Darrow regarding the origins of his success. Darrow claimed that the day he started down the path toward significant success was the day he went to get a mortgage for $2,000 to buy a home. The lender's wife spoke up and said, "Don't be a fool. He'll never make enough money to pay it off." Though Darrow himself had serious doubts about whether he could pay it off, something inside happened when he heard her remark. It made him so furious and determined that he demanded success and achievement from that day forward. That's exactly what I mean by embracing radical responsibility.

Now this by no means eliminates the need for a relationship with a higher power, but it does mean that *we* are ultimately in control of building and strengthening that relationship. Again, as we embrace each of these behaviors, life just gets more and more exciting as the possibilities unveil themselves.

Within you right now is the power and ability to take the necessary action to be successful and fulfilled in every area of your life. You can do it, you are worthy of it, and you do deserve it, but you must take responsibility for it.

Pro-Tip: Challenging Limiting Beliefs

It's time to have a deep and honest discussion with yourself. Are there any problems in your life that remain unsolved because at some point you labeled them unsolvable? If so, take a new look at them rationally and challenge that belief. Ask: Why do I believe I can't? Why do I believe it's not possible? Are these beliefs based on real evidence or just assumptions? Could I be incorrect in these beliefs? If I were looking at another person in a similar situation, would I come to the same conclusion? Push yourself to challenge any limiting beliefs you may have.

Mind Your Posture

In the late 1960s, a young PhD student by the name of Carol Dweck[13] was studying helplessness and children. She wanted to understand why some children give up when faced with challenges while other children are motivated by them. She found that the kids who gave up easily also avoided challenges and felt threatened by those who were different from themselves. They viewed growth and learning as things outside of their control. Dweck calls this approach to life a *fixed mindset*.

The other group of children, who accepted and embraced challenges and were motivated to overcome them, felt that with hard work they could accomplish just about anything. They didn't see their innate abilities as "fixed" but rather as gifts that may be improved with practice over time. These kids were labeled as having a *growth mindset*.

To study the differences, Dweck tracked the performance of a group of seventh-grade students for two years. She found that those with the growth mindset progressed significantly faster academically than their fixed-mindset peers. The growth-mindset students pushed themselves harder and sought out challenges that were just barely within their current abilities, and they even viewed failures in which they learned something as positive. The fixed-mindset students avoided challenges and quit when things became difficult.

What's interesting here is that the only real difference between the growth-minded students and the fixed-minded students was their inherent posture toward the world and their circumstances. The growth-mindset students embraced radical responsibility for their improvement whereas the fixed-mindset students had a posture of

---

13   For a recent overview of Dweck's mindset research, see Carol Dweck: Praising Intelligence: Costs to Children's Self-Esteem and Motivation, *The Bing Times*, November 1, 2007, https://bingschool.stanford.edu/news/carol-dweck-praising-intelligence-costs-children-s-self-esteem-and-motivation.

victimhood and blame—and, frankly, fear and timidity. These early studies have now been followed by years of research that shows how people with a fixed mindset have lower self-esteem and struggle in life. The only shift that mattered was the decision to embrace responsibility, and it made all the difference.

Another great example from scientific literature comes from Dr. Kelly McGonigal's work out of Stanford University. In her book *The Upside of Stress*[14] she explains that how we view stress makes a huge impact on how stress influences us. Specifically, those who view stressors as "challenges" rather than "threats" by focusing on what can be controlled display a decrease in negative emotions such as anxiety and fear. This in turn allows them to thrive in the midst of stress. But perhaps the most interesting benefit about your mindset toward stress is a biological one.

Two hormones are at play during stress, namely cortisol and DHEA. Over time, chronically elevated cortisol levels create lingering inflammation, depression, and poor immune function. By contrast, DHEA has been linked to reduction in anxiety, depression, and even heart disease. People who release more DHEA than cortisol when under stress are said to have a high "growth index of stress" and many associated health benefits. The only difference in a high vs. low growth index of stress is whether a person chooses to view the stress as a welcome challenge or an unwanted threat. Richard Florida[15] performed a poll of twenty thousand creative professionals and gave them the choice of 38 different factors as motivators to do their best work. The number one overall factor chosen was *challenge and responsibility*.

---

14   McGonigal, Dr. Kelly. *The Upside of Stress*, New York: Avery, 2015.

15   Richard Florida is the author of two interesting books: *The Rise of the Creative Class* (New York: Basic Boos, 2002) and more recently *The New Urban Crisis: How Our Cities Are Increasing Inequality, Deepening Segregation, and Failing the Middle Class—and What We Can Do About It*, New York: Basic Books, 2017.

As an aspiring Top 1% performer, begin to view stress as a challenge with a proactive focus on growth as opposed to any sort of threat. Go ahead and stop now, and verbally and on paper state that you embrace radical responsibility for your mindset toward stress. Do it now.

We all have this built-in equality filter that serves as a major weakness in our lives. The quicker we can understand that things aren't just and equal all the time, the easier it will be to embrace radical responsibility in every area of our lives.

Grasping this concept is a true differentiator. Realize that everything you are doing in life to reach the Top 1% involves creating a radical amount of value for those around you. This process is inherently "unfair." But the key is that worrying about equality and fairness and even justice more than you care about the value creation piece is what keeps you in mediocrity. Success is a long-term game, and the majority of the 99% are stuck in short-term understanding and practice. Short-term thinking and short-term action are habitual sicknesses that trap us in our current level of thinking and achievement, and ultimately wealth. We have to find a cure for this conundrum. The experts have been studying this solution for years.

The Magic Pill Is Really PIL

What if there were a magic pill that research has shown could add years to your life, reduce the risk of Alzheimer's by more than 50%, diminish inflammation in your body, reduce your risk of heart attack and stroke, and repair your DNA? And what if that magic pill also made you happier and gave you better sex? Well, this magic does exist, but it's not a *pill*—it's *PIL*. The magic is *purpose in life* (PIL).[16]

---

16   E.S. Kim, J.K. Sun, N. Park, and C. Peterson, "purpose in life and reduced incidence of stroke in older adults: the health and retirement study," *Journal of Psychosomatic Research* 74 (2013): 427-32; P.A. Boyle, A.S. Buchman, R.S. Wilson, L. You, J.A. Schneider, and D.A. Bennett, "Effect of purpose in life on

George Bernard Shaw said, "This is the true joy in life, the being used for a purpose recognized by yourself as a mighty one...the being a force of nature instead of a feverish selfish little clod of ailments and grievances."

Perhaps the greatest responsibility you have in life is to take the time necessary to cultivate a carefully crafted life purpose. To be clear, purpose in life is concerned with what you most deeply value and *what matters most.*

For inspiration, here's mine: "To reduce the suffering of others, turn their doubt into power, contribute with generosity, and deliver the hope of a future without limitation through compassionate mentoring."

This purpose will define who you are and serve as your unique intrinsic motivator.

You're likely familiar with Jim Collin's book *Good to Great.*[17] He breaks down a group of companies based on their managerial and financial excellence to analyze what makes a "great" company. But you may be less familiar with a book called *Firms of Endearment,*[18] written by a group of business school professors, that identified twenty-eight companies based solely on the strength of and dedication to a revenue-transcending purpose.

The authors matched the financial performance over fifteen years of their twenty-eight firms of endearment against the S&P 500, and a group of companies selected from *Good to Great.* The study found that over the first three years, the *Good to Great* companies more than doubled the performance of the firms of endearment and the S&P 500 companies.

---

the relation between Alzheimer's disease pathologic changes on cognitive function in advanced age," *Archives In General Psychiatry* 69, no. 5 (2012): 499-505; A.M. Wood and S. Joseph "The Absence of Positive Psychological (Eudemonic) Well-Being as a risk factor for depression: A 10-year cohort study," *Journal of Affective Disorders* 122, 2010, pp. 213-217.

17 Collins, Jim. *Good to Great*, New York: Harper Business, 2001.

18 Sisodia, R., D.B. Wolf, and J. Sheth. *Firms of Endearment*, Upper Saddle River, NJ: Prentice Hall, 2014.

But, over the full fifteen years, the firms of endearment ended up returning 1,681% of investment compared to the 263% of investment returned by the *Good to Great* companies. The S&P 500 were a distant third at 118% return. This shows that in the same way purpose among individuals brings incredible return, it also rings true in business. From this individual study, over the long term, a revenue-transcending purpose appears far more important than simply managerial and financial skill. *To support this, a 2013 Gallup study found that the number one way to minimize employee disengagement is to focus diligently on the organization's purpose.*[19]

Pro-Tip: 5-Step Approach to Creating Your PIL (Purpose in Life)

1. *Compile the three to four answers from your exercise: Top 1% ID Part I (These are your deepest-held inspirational drivers).*
2. *Contemplate and answer the question: "What do I want people to say about me at my funeral?"*
3. *Answer the question: "What are the long-term goals in my life that matter most?"*
4. *Put these pieces together into a PIL statement.*
5. *Post your PIL statement where you'll see it daily. Memorize it and share it with those close to you.*

Radical responsibility is 100% about setting a set of personal standards that are sacred for you. Do you want to be perceived as a pro in every area of your life? The way to do this is to make integrity and responsibility (via quality, consistency, and timeliness) non-negotiable.

Take total personal accountability for the value you create and the results you get regardless of all other circumstances. Radical responsibility also requires you to get clear on what's motivating you on

---

19   See https://www.slideshare.net/InnoGarage/state-of-the-global-workplace-report-2013-by-gallup.

this journey to becoming a Shepherd Leader and Top 1% performer. I call these inspirational drivers, and you will return to them again and again throughout this book. Here is an exercise to help you identify them for yourself:

EXERCISE: Top 1% ID Part I

Answer each of the following questions as thoroughly as possible. It's totally okay if there are repeat answers across multiple questions—you'll see why after you answer the questions.

- *How do you like to fill your time?* It's a simple fact of human nature that people make time for the things that are MOST important to them and RUN OUT of time for the things that don't matter to them on a deep level. So how is your time spent?
- *How do you spend your money?* You somehow find the money or resources for the things that are deeply important priorities in your life and can't afford the things that aren't. So how do you spend your money?
- *What gives you energy?* The activities we dread rob us of energy and vitality whereas the activities that are our inspirational drivers give us energy. So what activities give you energy rather than take it from you?
- *In what areas are you most consistently disciplined?* What are the things you reliably do without needing any external pressure or motivation? You can't stop yourself from doing these activities because you're so driven by them.
- *What do you think about most of the time?* These aren't crazy fantasies but rather meaningful goals that are gradually moving toward accomplishment. What are the most frequent thoughts you have about how you want your life to be?
- *What do you absolutely love to learn about?* What types of movies or documentaries do you gravitate toward? What

types of books do you consistently read, and what types of magazines do you browse in airport bookstores? What could you learn about forever and never get enough?

- *What things fill your personal or office space?* Do you have lots of pictures of loved ones or artwork or photos of famous people? Do you have personal awards or documented achievements? Or do you have lots of books or journals? What types of books are they? What things mean so much to you that you'd never put them in storage because you want them around at all times?

Now go back through and find the answers that are most often repeated and record how many times they repeat. Find the answer repeated most often, followed by the second most and the third most. Based on these rankings, you'll now have a list of your top three or four strongest drivers.

Behavior #1 offers you a meaningful path to embrace the concept of radical responsibility. You are the keeper of your fate, and embracing challenges is part of your existence. As you trade practices that create a victim mentality for those that support responsibility, it will allow you to forge ahead and manifest a meaningful life of abundance. In the next chapter we will focus on Behavior #2, which falls squarely on recognizing and optimizing your higher self.

Chapter 3

BEHAVIOR #2:
RECOGNIZE AND OPTIMIZE YOUR HIGHER SELF

One can have no smaller or greater mastery
than mastery of oneself.
~ Leonardo da Vinci ~

Have you ever felt like you were battling a constant loop of mental noise and internal judgment? This self-sabotaging internal monologue filled with doubt and limitation has the power to ruin your life and devastate your true potential. We all experience it, in varying degrees of intensity and presence. You may not be sure how much of it is true or whether you even believe it, but you spend your time trying to break through the noise, overcome the stress and perceived limitations, and somehow transcend the insecurity to rise to the elite level. Negative, undisciplined thinking sabotages achievement in the short term and destroys the possibility for success and impact in the long term.

We all have a little voice inside our heads driven by fear. Seth Godin calls it the *lizard brain*, my friend Tim Alison calls it *the voice*, and Steven Pressfield calls it *the resistance*. I like to call it the *primal self*. Everyone has this voice, and its job is to keep you in Mediocrity. Unfortunately, the *primal self* has an incredible ability to disguise mediocrity as safety, so you think it's doing you a favor.

You see, when you perceive danger, your sympathetic nervous system turns on, your body mobilizes energy, and it activates the "fight-or-flight" response. The acute stress response helps you to respond to threats, dangers, and other risks to your survival and is certainly not a bad thing. But the response can't differentiate between a case of road rage in five o'clock traffic, an argument with your significant other, or a face-to-face encounter with a grizzly bear. It is either on or off.

Here's how it works in a nutshell. Your brain is wired to process incoming information and screen for threats. This happens in a structure called the amygdala, located in the temporal lobes.

The difference between human beings and other animals is that *thinking* enables us to turn this fight-or-flight mechanism on. Our thoughts alone can create a fight-or-flight scenario. And, even worse, the thought trigger does not need to be related to anything in your present circumstances. It can be about something in the past, or more often some hypothetical future event. Most disastrous is how we have the ability to turn short-term stressful situations into long-term responses. No living organism was designed to deal with the negative consequences on the body that take place when the acute stress response remains on for a long duration and high frequency. Our body breaks down, depletes our immune system due to a lack of energy for growth and repair, our genes become less regulated, and we experience disease. The fact is, fear, worry, and anxiety create the same chemicals in your body as those created when a wild animal is chasing after you. This is no way to live.

The turning point for you (as it has been for me) will be to *recognize* that you have TWO selves operating at all times. You can almost think of these as two identities competing for your mental energy. I refer to the two selves as the *primal self* and the *higher self*. In simplest terms, the *primal self* is your "false identity" and the *higher self* is your "true identity."

The primal self has something to prove. It has immense needs for security that must be met. The higher self is infinitely powerful and needs no external validation. The primal self needs to assert itself and show dominance. The higher self is confident yet humble. It has real power, and when you have real power you don't need to show off your power. The primal self is needy and lacking. It always fears loss and failure because reputation, money, and good looks is all it has. The higher self is inherently generous because it knows it will never be less by giving some away. It knows no limitation because truly spiritual gifts (generosity, forgiveness, service, kindness, patience) only multiply when given away. The primal self is small, insecure ego. The higher self is infinite in all ways.

The primal self is the undisciplined mind that leads to the Mayhem level of performance I described in the first chapter. It's a sense of chaos and turmoil that makes optimal performance an impossibility. The primal self despises the things that bring about Mastery most readily, namely deep focus and deep authenticity. The primal self wants you to stay superficial, unfocused, and ego-driven.

On the other hand, the higher self is the calm, steady ally that is ready to take you to Mastery. Interestingly, the root of the word "discipline" means to be a disciple to something higher than yourself. This higher self is our divine nature, which is capable of more than you can imagine.

The primal self is characterized most by fear—fear of judgment, fear of failing, fear of poverty, fear of underachievement, and ultimately fear of death. What if I get kicked out of the group (i.e., family, religion, race, nation, or peer group)? Your primal self is a disgusting, egotistical narcissist. Mine is too. It thinks only of scarcity, competition, and comparison with others.

The primal self is nothing more than your brain. Your brain can be described as three mini-brains put together. The most primitive mini-brain is often called the *reptilian brain* and is made up of the brainstem and cerebellum. This part regulates basic life functions such as heart rate, breathing, and coordination. Subconscious in nature, it is completely on auto-drive whether you are thinking about something or not.

The *mammalian brain*, or second mini-brain, regulates the acute stress response as well as the need to eat and reproduce. It's also responsible for emotions, hormonal balance, and sleep regulation.

The third and final part of the primal self is the *neocortex*, which houses our nearly unlimited potential. This is where reasoning, planning, and learning take place. The neocortex is almost infinitely powerful, but it still needs a director.

That director is independent of your brain and is known as your higher self. This higher self transcends the matter and function of your brain and has the ability to run the show. It's very difficult to describe what it feels like to experience the higher self. But one thing I think everyone has experienced at least once is the sensation of being moved to tears by a piece of music. I'm not sure what music that is for you, but to this day, if I allow myself to sit and listen to the classic hymn "It Is Well with My Soul," I get emotional. That feeling of "the touching of your soul" is you coming into contact with your higher self. That's what I'm talking about.

Each of us has both of these selves simultaneously, and an epic battle is being fought between the two at all times—the battle between what we know "ought to be done" and what feels and looks good in the immediate short term.

The higher self allows you to step outside of the powerful primal self and evaluate (on a higher level) the ideal behaviors you know you must integrate into your life to become the person you desire to be. It allows you to reach a kind of silence in your mind that can help you witness your brain in action from a third-party perspective. And this way you can separate your identity from the thoughts that come into your mind and tap into the power of the higher self to watch and evaluate those thoughts. This type of thinking takes place in the cerebral cortex, and it appears to be available to us as human beings more than any other species because of the plasticity of our brains.

As you'll see throughout this book, the visions you create and pursue, the goals you set, and the behaviors you adopt literally change the connections and wiring in your brain. This gives you immense power if you're willing to embrace it. The key is to recognize the power of the higher self and accept the responsibility (see Behavior #1) of optimizing this power to create an ideal life. The higher self is also where spiritual connection takes place. Specifically, scientists are finding that this spiritual center seems to be located in the parietal cortex region of the brain. The key point here is that the higher self is not limited by physical and material circumstances but often relies on a deep faith and a controlled state of powerful emotion along with strategic planning to bring about your desired reality.

As you become more aware of this dichotomy, you'll notice the constant tendency of your thinking toward negativity. This is because your primal self, which is the default self, is wired with a bias toward survival-orientation. It decides and acts on life-threatening scenarios every day and is conditioned to be fearful and pessimistic. In many ways your primal self creates so much fear and false storytelling in your own mind that it's difficult to view yourself from the perspective of objective reality.

To quote the late Steve Jobs, it's a "reality distortion field," but in this case not the good kind. The better you become at witnessing your thoughts and tapping into your higher self, the more aware you'll be of how weak your mind is if not optimized effectively. The key here is to use your awareness of the negative thinking as a trigger to immediately prompt your mind into optimized thinking and performance.

That is why Behavior #2, which is recognizing and optimizing your higher self, is crucial to operating in your Top 1% potential. We are all subject to the challenges and pre-conditioning of our mind. However, how we understand and associate with the tremendous influence our mind has upon us can almost certainly open otherwise unlocked doors.

Pro-Tip: Personal Performance Manipulation

When you feel certain negative emotions such as anxiety, fear, doubt, or guilt rushing through your body, immediately recognize those emotions, call them out, and make an announcement to yourself that says, "I guess this is the primal self taking over, and all I have to do here is shut it down, refocus my energy, and understand I can choose for my higher self to regain control." It's a very subtle shift in energy and recognizing when the nasty primal emotions are trying to push their way through and take over. You don't have to let that happen. Just call them what they are and decide that your higher self—that version of you that is more highly evolved, wise, and spiritually connected—is going to take over again.

Addicted to Stress?

Your higher self is always under attack. Whether it be through internal or external forces, we should always remain in a protective state of mind, trying to maintain consistency and efficiency in how we think and what we allow in our lives. Perhaps one of the greatest enemies to our growth and development, stress, is at play. Psychologically, over-production of stress hormones like cortisol and adrenaline promotes the emotions of fear, anger, frustration, aggression, insecurity, and even guilt. These chemicals also cause elevated blood pressure, heart rate, and rapid breathing. Most people spend a large portion of their time thinking these types of negative thoughts and thus live in a state of Mayhem.

As much of a threat that stress can be on your operating system, you also have control over how you manage the body's relationship to stress. Stress is neither inherently "good" or "bad." Each of us will be confronted by stress every day. The key is in how we manage our relationship to the stress. Distress is the negative label put on stress that is unexpected. When used intentionally, stress can be good (eustress) and is essential for growth. The classic example of this is weight training to build muscle. Muscle tissue is broken down by submission to high levels of stress, and then new muscle tissue equipped for higher levels of stress is developed. Stress is stress, but the story you create in your mind about how you view the stress is the key component.

For example, imagine you are feeling a moment of stress. How would you normally respond? Likely in allowing the feeling of stress to overtake and then overwhelm your mind and body. But it doesn't have to be that way. There are a number of ways to deflect stress. One such way is through quadrant breathing.

The average person takes fourteen to fifteen breaths per minute and uses a third of their lung capacity. This raises blood pressure, causes carbon dioxide buildup, and fosters an undisciplined mind. A well-trained performer, on the other hand, will take three to five breaths per minute. Though often not taught in the West, breath control is an easy and effective way to boost energy, focus your mind, and gain a sense of calm. When you practice controlled breathing, you slow your heart rate and regulate your autonomic nervous system. Here are the simple steps you can take to effectuate this goal:

1. Utilize your higher self to observe how a stressor is affecting your mind and body. (negative thinking, heart rate increase, rapid breathing, etc.)
2. Immediately cut the negative labeling of the stressor off with some kind of statement of confidence. (mine is "Stay focused")
3. Shift your label of the stress to a positive one. (i.e., "Wow, I have a rush of energy")
4. Employ quadrant breathing.

Quadrant Breathing

Do this ideally once a day for three to five minutes, but especially before high-stress situations.

1. Exhale all the air from your lungs.
2. Inhale to a count of five.
3. Retain and hold for a count of five.
4. Exhale slowly to a count of five.
5. Hold after exhaling for a count of five.

Focused breathing gives you a point of concentration that immediately reduces stress and enhances your sense of self-control as well as your ability to make decisions in the midst of fear or chaos. It's an effective tool, whether you're looking for enhanced performance in your leadership, in the operating room, or while delivering a presentation

Powerful Emotions, Powerful Results

Psychological forces are never one-dimensional in their value. For example, anger and aggression can actually be used to motivate, overcome the forces of evil and tyranny, and, in the case of my mission, speak truth into the lives of those who are stuck in mediocrity. The term I use for this channeling of primal emotion into higher emotion is "controlled rage." Make no mistake, we all have a dark side and are capable of very evil things.

As the great Russian writer Alexander Solzhenitsyn suggested, the line dividing good and evil cuts through the heart of every human being. But what's beautiful is how we also have the capacity to use these inherent human characteristics as the "controlled rage" that will decrease fear and self-doubt and increase self-confidence and self-respect. There's only a *very* subtle shift between your inherent capacity for destructive behavior and your ability to operate with unshakable virtue. The shift is from primal self to higher self, and it's a moment-to-moment decision.

A common mistake we all make is to think of ourselves as physical beings with a spiritual side, but it's much more accurate and useful to understand ourselves as *spiritual beings with a physical body*—and the ability to use our thinking to alter present and future situations.

When we become the materialistic physical self, living in fear, we get this backwards. As you'll learn, the quantum level of reality defines everything on the fundamental level as energy. We know that energy has different frequencies and wavelengths. When we're focused on our physical material being primarily, our emotional resilience falls to a lower (primal self) level. In contrast, as we move up the emotional resilience hierarchy we move closer to our true spiritual identity and closer to the ideal operating conditions our Creator bestowed upon us (higher self).

Here's something bizarre, but generally true about us. We become addicted to our problems and our stress. It's true. The bad jobs, bad relationships, and bad thinking literally get us high!

Our thoughts and feelings, which tend to be centered around self-doubt and limitation, pull us toward our problems, stressors, and poor decisions. We clutch tightly to this low-energy thinking because it reaffirms our limited material identity to us. At this point we feel like Mayhem is too much to overcome because the negative feedback loop is so strong and limited thinking so primal that the only thing we care about is self-preservation.

This is the ultimate egocentric behavior because we begin to obsess about our bodies and the details of our physical environment to the point where we feel powerless to change. Self-indulgence, self-importance, self-centeredness, and ultimately self-hatred take over. I'm fascinated and troubled by how so many of the world's most renowned (and many of my favorite) performers, several of them at the pinnacle in their careers, take their own lives. Kurt Cobain, Chris Cornell, Anthony Bourdain, Robin Williams, Kate Spade, and on and on and on. When I study these lives, I can't help but feel strongly that the common denominator is the lack of recognition and optimization of the higher self.

Every thought you have produces a chemical. If you think different thoughts, the connections in your brain fire in specific patterns and combinations, which then produce specific neurotransmitters with the exact signature that matches the thoughts, so your body will feel the way you are thinking. It's like this cascade where neurotransmitters help neurons speak to one another, which then causes neuropeptides to be released and subsequently drive specific hormones to be upregulated.

So when you have negative or fearful thoughts, it only takes a matter of seconds for your body to feel anxious or agitated. On the flipside, when you have empowering, goal-oriented, confident, or even joyous thoughts, the chemicals produced will make you feel joyful and successful. This creates a positive feedback loop, so as we start to feel the way we're thinking, we'll then begin to think the way we are feeling. This is why it's so crucial to monitor and take control of our thoughts on a moment-to-moment basis. They are literally shaping the composition of our body, as well as our physical, mental, and spiritual identity. This identity then produces effects in our life.

Albert Ellis, one of the forefathers of modern psychology, found that how we think and talk about our experiences heavily influences the way we feel about them. In other words, our thoughts are intimately connected with our emotions. He also found that what we think is often irrational. The subtle remarks we make in our own minds such as "I'm such an idiot" or "My life is over" lead to underlying emotions like frustration, irritability, anger, and even hopelessness. This irrational talk in our heads makes life infinitely more difficult than necessary. Unfortunately, we've become so used to hearing this critical voice in our minds that we become hypnotized and don't even realize it's happening.

Years of thinking that specific pattern of thoughts, and then feeling feelings that match those thoughts, creates a hardwired state of being we define as "who we are." This is where it's easy to fall into labeling ourselves with negatives such as "I am lazy" or "I am anxious" or "I am stupid." The key step here is to begin to think greater than that pre-programmed state of feeling that has developed. Studies show that nearly 95% of the person you are by middle age is directed by a series of automatic subconscious programs. These programs include things such as self-doubt, worry, judgment, driving a car, taking care of our bodies or not, overeating, and blaming others. In many ways we're asleep at the wheel, and these programs operate all but 5% of our activity.

When you make the decision to regain control of the situation through goal setting and strategic planning, this internal programming will come up with a number of reasons why it's crazy for you to try to break out of the habit of creating negative identities. It will dwell on and highlight all your weaknesses and negative traits. It will catastrophize and create worst-case scenarios in your mind about what could happen because of the change in the internal chemistry that's being made, effectively throwing the body into a state of Mayhem. This hardwired programming has to be broken down and rewired into a new set of patterns based on the exact identity you want to have, and the exact person you desire to be.

My Personal Battle

Earlier I mentioned my own battle with anxiety and self-doubt. For much of my life, I experienced a lack of self-worth that created this chemical makeup. Eventually I realized you can substitute any negative thought pattern you might deal with. Remember, chemistry works the same way. So, whether it's anxiety, depression, guilt, shame, laziness, or victimhood, the outcome will be the chemistry in your body conforming to the individual thinking pattern.

Here's how it goes: after multiple years of repeatedly thinking "I'm not good enough," I had created an environment of anxiety and doubt. Every time I had an anxious thought, my mind sent a signal to my body to produce the specific neurotransmitters and hormones that make up the feelings of fear and anxiety. This came to feel very familiar.

Having done this so many times, the cell membranes of my individual cells adapted receptor sites for these chemicals associated with fear and anxiety and doubt, for easy processing. Over time, the cells become so desensitized to this painful chemistry of anxiety in the body that an addiction develops *at the cellular level*. This addiction kills. In my case, any time anything went wrong, or slightly less than perfect, my automatic assumption was that the world was crashing down, it was my fault, and *I knew I wasn't good enough*. On a subconscious level, I had become anxious most of the time, and my body had become an outward expression of anxiety and self-doubt.

The body becomes addicted to these negative emotions in the same way it becomes addicted to drugs.[20] So trying to change these deep-seated patterns of emotion is like going through drug withdrawal. Your brain has conditioned your body to expect one particular signal or several signals based on the pattern of anxiety and self-doubt, and as you introduce an active process of calmness and confidence, an alarm goes off and the cells begin to rebel. Immediately the cells send a message directly up the spinal cord to the brain. This process takes seconds.

At the exact same time, the hypothalamus in the brain, which serves as a sort of thermostat to maintain homeostasis in the body, signals the chemicals in the bloodstream to down-regulate accordingly to allow for the more familiar emotional state. The body desperately wants us to return to our familiar primal selves, so it activates the networks of neurons that have fired and wired together for years and produced these familiar chemical outcomes. This is when we begin to feel things like procrastination, laziness, and complacency.

---

20   Sapolsky, Robert M. *Why Zebras Don't Get Ulcers*, New York: Henry Holt and Company, 2004.

In other words, it "feels" better to give up on trying to change your thoughts and emotional patterns. This is also when the mind will try to sabotage you by bringing up past events and memories that reaffirm your feelings of anxiety, inadequacy, guilt, shame, or whatever the battle is for you. Breaking down the physiology of this process makes it easy to understand why your primal self is so powerful.

Pro-Tip: Higher-Self Redirect

Here's a three-step process I've come up with called the Higher-Self Redirect that has given me much more control over my thinking and has helped others to do the same. Here are the three steps:

1. *Notice and become consciously aware of the weak, negative thought.*
2. *Cut the thought off with a statement of confidence that resonates with you personally (e.g., "Come on"; "You've got this"; my personal favorite is "Stay focused").*
3. *Anchor your new positive thought state with a mantra or song that has meaning and positive emotion for you personally (mine is "Don't Stop Me Now" by Queen).*

The specific choice of the statement and mantra or song is not important. However, they must have meaning to you in some way that is associated with positive emotion so they will engage your mind. Ideally, with discipline, you'll be able to redirect to your higher self with little resistance as your song and confidence statement will be constantly at hand.

Everything Is Energy

We've all got a huge amount of energy built up inside us. It needs to go somewhere. This energy, in many ways, can be channeled in negative directions or positive ones. That's where controlling our thoughts comes into play. For example, when you wake up in the morning on the wrong side of the bed, and all you want to do is kick the dog, that's likely a result of your negative energy desiring expression, and it's coming from somewhere. Something is driving it, whether it was as simple as a bad dream the night before, an issue at work you're dealing with, a fight with your spouse, or your own self-condemnation. Some dissatisfaction or inner turmoil is churning in your subconscious, and you need to pinpoint it because until you do you can't move that energy to a positive direction—and it will leak out or even explode. As you'll see throughout this book, *everything is energy*, and it matters how you are channeling yours.

This is really a spiritual issue. If you're disconnected from your divine Creator, which we all are until we reconnect through enlightenment or salvation or whatever term you use for it, these negative energy patterns (commonly called *sin*) will dominate your life. And your primal self will drive your behavior.

Pro-Tip: Daily Success Diary

Finish each day with a success diary session. Take five to ten minutes each night prior to sleep to review all the things that went well throughout the course of that day. This will do wonders for your mental health and energy level. As we take note of the things that went well during our day, we can then elevate our level of gratitude and focus on the positive. Reflect on the negative noise and allow your mind to wash it away, giving you a clear path to a peaceful, calm rest.

Winston Churchill was a man of great discipline and great passion. He believed in virtue, loved reading and studying, and was a dedicated soldier. Though he is said to have been born with a feeble body, he built up such a powerful and determined mind and spirit that his physical limitations became irrelevant. As a war correspondent in South Africa, he was taken prisoner in 1899 and barely survived. Shortly thereafter, he was elected to his first political office in 1900. He married his wife, Clementine, at age thirty-three and published seven books before the end of WWI. He was prone to over-commitment and overspending, so he certainly was not perfect, and his life was characterized by mistakes and lapses of judgment. Nevertheless, by the mid-1920s Churchill served as chancellor of the exchequer and produced a six-volume account of WWI called *The World in Crisis*. Churchill's example is a clear testament to what's possible when energy is consistently channeled toward recognizing and optimizing the higher self.

Each of us will face crises in our lives. In fact, it's likely we'll face many of them. A painful divorce, the loss of a job, a failed business, the debilitating loss of a loved one, or a devastating diagnosis. These scenarios will require our very best mental and emotional responses to rise to the occasion and "handle" the situation. In a world with so much pain and stress, how do we control our responses, stay cool, and perform at our very best?

As you'll see, it requires much more than sheer willpower to master self-control. Actually, though you often don't realize it, your EMOTIONS are instrumental in your decision making and actions. You are driven to action *exclusively* by emotion. Emotion drives the body to act, and action ignites emotional energy. The two are tightly interwoven.

The Antidote

If you ignore your higher self in favor of your primal self, you'll become totally self-centered and out of control. If your primal self is allowed to dictate all decisions, then no amount of pleasure will ever be enough to satisfy you. This ultimately leads to a quiet life of desperation.

At the same time, denying your primal self is not a good practice either. You become numb, disconnected, and indifferent if you reject your emotions and feelings. New relationships will suffer, and it will be very difficult to find meaning.

A study focused on the effects of self-transcendence on neural responses to persuasive messages and health behavior change and published in the National Academy of Sciences used functional MRI scans to examine what happens in the brain when people are presented with threatening messages, or stimuli that cause a stress response. In this study, by thinking deeply about their core values, they were able to override the threatening stimuli. Individuals asked to think deeply about their core values before they received a threatening message showed an increase in the neural activity in a part of the brain associated with "positive valuation." In simple terms it just means these people were overriding their primal instincts, and instead of shutting down when faced with a threat, their brains accepted and moved toward the challenge presented to them.[21]

Interestingly, these findings weren't just happening in the lab. The individuals who reflected on their values went on to overcome fears in their lives at a much higher rate than the control group, who were given the threats without reflecting on their core values first. This really makes sense because in situations that seem scary or overwhelming, our primal self automatically tries to shut us down so we don't fail. It's protecting us from physical or emotional injury. However, the studies show that the less we think about ourselves and the more we think about a transcendent purpose that is aligned with our core values, the more our higher self shows up and the better we perform.

Dr. Angela Duckworth, who coined the term "grit" and wrote a landmark bestselling book by the same name,[22] suggests that grit is a hallmark of high achievers in every domain. It's the reason why some people persevere when others quit. Duckworth has found that grit is

21 Effects of self-transcendence on neural responses to persuasive messages and health behavior change Yoona Kang, Nicole Cooper, Prateekshit Pandey, Christin Scholz, Matthew Brook O'Donnell, Matthew D. Lieberman, Shelley E. Taylor, Victor J. Strecher, Sonya Dal Cin, Sara Konrath, Thad A. Polk, Kenneth Resnicow, Lawrence An, Emily B. Falk Proceedings of the National Academy of Sciences Oct 2018, 115 (40) 9974-9979; DOI: 10.1073/pnas.1805573115

22 Duckworth, Angela. *Grit: The Power of Passion and Perseverance*, New York: Scribner, 2016.

not an innate ability but one that can be cultivated over time. She has found that, along with passion (a deep and profound interest in something), grit is often accompanied by a strong sense of purpose. Gritty people draw upon a greater cause for inspiration and perseverance.

The key of course is to recognize and optimize your higher self. You can then use it as a tool. You must accept the power of emotions and channel them in a way that works for you rather than against you. The best way to do this is what is referred to in psychology as "emotional regulation."

This essentially amounts to aligning your higher self with your primal self. In other words, you align your ability to think with your cerebral cortex with the powerful emotions driven by your primal brain to get a synergistic effect. How is this done? By getting very clear on your personal values and motivations. There is a quick exercise you can go through to get a good idea of what these *inspirational drivers* are for you (I use the term Top 1% ID as an abbreviation). In the previous chapter you completed the first part of Top 1% ID; now it's time to expand it a little further.

The Identity Loop

The Shepherd Leader Identity Loop is a positive feedback system that starts with your innate inspirational drivers. Here is a visual of the loop:

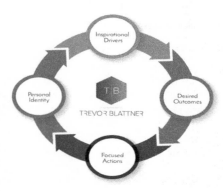

The initial step in the identity loop is discovering your *inspirational drivers*. Your inspirational drivers dictate, or lead to, your *desired outcomes*, which is the second stop on the identity loop. The desired outcomes are emotional goals and aspirations you want to achieve that are connected deeply to your innate inspirational drivers. The desired outcomes are emotionally charged, which is essential. These desired outcomes are things you're very passionate about and are connected to your mission and purpose in life.

Your inspirational drivers will dictate and lead to your desired outcomes, which will then lead to the third stop on the identity loop, your *focused actions*. Your focused actions are the things you strategically plan out that you know must be done and the tasks that need to be performed to bring your desired outcomes into reality. So your emotionally charged desired outcomes drive your focused actions. This is why your emotions and your actions are so deeply intertwined. They are intertwined on the subconscious level often without you knowing it, but when you understand this you can actually use it to your advantage and plan for it, which is what your goal is throughout this process.

Finally, the fourth step or stop on the identity loop is your *personal identity* because ultimately your actions—the things you *do* in life—create the person you become. Just as your overall choices dictate who you are and where you are in life, the actions you choose to take create your reality and your identity. Your personal identity will then feed back into your inspirational drivers, and the loop continues throughout your life.

As you study the loop, it will become evident that you do have control over this process. In fact, as you become more aware of it and more adept at controlling it, you can literally *change who you are* over time. And this is precisely the point: to choose who you want to be and become that person. The identity loop is simply a graphic representation of this process, and it should be helpful as you create your path to the Top 1%.

Pro-Tip: Leveraging Your Prefrontal Cortex

The prefrontal cortex, a subsection of the neo cortex responsible for conscious thinking, has a lot in common with muscle because it requires a lot of energy to function well. It gets tired from use and requires adequate rest to do its best work. This is why making difficult decisions is impossible when you're tired but may take just a minute or two when you're well rested. Also, deep thinking requires large amounts of energy, as does visualizing, prioritizing your hierarchy of tasks, and planning for the future. The solution is to rethink the way you value and use your prefrontal cortex to make it optimized for performance. Here are three practices to put in place:

1. *Take time to prioritize your most important tasks when your energy level is at its highest (usually first thing in the morning or after a workout). Prioritize in a way that puts activities aligned with your Top 1% ID and PIL statement at the top.*

2. *Create visuals for complex ideas rather than keeping them in your mind. Get information that's in your head onto a whiteboard or a piece of paper so it's out in the world and not taking up space in your mind. Getting things out of your head will free up massive amounts of vital energy for you.*

3. *Avoid high-energy-burning conscious activities such as dealing with email until after deep thinking, prioritizing, and strategizing (e.g., consider devoting forty-five minutes of every hour on high-energy thinking, reserving ten minutes to see if any emails are urgent, and five minutes resting your mind) because email will drain you very quickly if not dealt with strategically.*

What Fear Really Is

Remember, *everything you're afraid of is based on a feeling. All fears are based on either emotional or physical situations that bring us the sensation of fear.* Write that down. Post it on your mirror. Post it on your computer screen. This concept has profound implications in every area of your life.

We've all suffered through some really horrible stuff. We may have gone through devastating breakups, physical and emotional abuse, failures of all kinds, bullying, and the loss of people who were important to us. And the bizarre yet universal thing is how we convince ourselves we deserve all this pain on some level. This is a very nasty emotional feeling of unworthiness and shame, which then sets the primal self up to reproduce this suffering (since it's driven by emotion). So it turns out not to be a lack of intellectual understanding that makes self-control such an overwhelming battle. It's actually because we have unintentionally trained our primal brains that we deserve pain and suffering.

Plastic surgeon Dr. Maxwell Maltz, in his book *Psycho-Cybernetics*, explains that the more he worked with his patients, the more convinced he became that what each of us really desires at the deepest level is more aliveness.[23] We want to live a life unrestricted by a poor self-image and self-imposed limitations. Success, achievement, and peace of mind are only experienced as *more life-force*. When we have more confidence and more success, we enjoy more life as it is meant to be lived.

Conversely, as you frustrate your God-given abilities and give in to fear, anxiety, and self-doubt, you lose your life-force and experience the pain associated with underachievement and lack of fulfillment. In fact, your self-image filters through all the goals you are setting for

---

23   Maltz, Maxwell. *Psycho-Cybernetics*, New York: TarcherPerigee, 2015.

yourself and attempting to convey to the goal-striving centers of your brain. If your self-image is incongruent with the vision and goals you are setting, then you have no chance of achieving those goals. But if you can alter your self-image and take it out of conflict with the goals, you can transcend those limitations and optimize your higher self.

Understand that living in your higher self 100% of the time is simply not possible (on this side of heaven). There's just too much inherent entropy in the universe for that. Complete order and complete Mastery will never come to pass. But this is a blessing because the process of growth and progress—but never complete Mastery—is where you find meaning. Some things are under your direct control and some are not. However, your response to all circumstances is within your realm of responsibility (review Behavior #1).

Pro-Tip: Avoid "Multitasking" Whenever Possible

MIT scientist and brain researcher Robert Desimone has discovered that the human brain is capable of holding only one visual concept in mind at any given time.[24] The ideal number of new ideas to try to understand at once seems to be just one. In addition, scientist Harold Pashler showed that when people do two cognitive tasks at one time, their cognitive ability can drop from that of a Harvard MBA to that of an eight-year-old. This phenomenon is called dual-task interference.[25]

One possible solution to this is using a concept called embedding. *This involves practicing very specific activities repeatedly until they become outsourced to a structure in your brain called the basal ganglia rather than being dealt with by the prefrontal cortex. Your basal ganglia recognize, store, and repeat patterns from your environment. These processes then become hardwired into your brain. This is why*

---

24   See https://cbmm.mit.edu/video/bob-desimone-visual-attention.

25   Pashler H., and Johnston J.C. Attentional limitations in dual-task performance. In: Pashler H., editor. *Attention*. Hove United Kingdom: Psychology Press/ Erlbaum, 1998, pp. 155–189.

you can drive, talk on the phone, and type while doing other activities. Here are a few suggestions on how to leverage these concepts:

1. *When you catch yourself trying to do two things at once that require conscious thinking, slow down and do one at a time.*

2. *Develop routines that can be repeated and embedded such as how you schedule your day, how you delete emails, and how you respond to routine emails.*

3. *Turn off your phone when you are doing focused work, or consider only having your phone on during select designated hours.*

4. *Only multitask (if you absolutely must) by combining embedded routines with active thinking tasks.*

Psychologically, overproduction of stress hormones like cortisol and adrenaline promotes the emotions of fear, anger, frustration, aggression, insecurity, and even guilt. These chemicals also cause elevated blood pressure, heart rate, and rapid breathing. Most people spend a large portion of their time thinking these types of negative thoughts and thus live in a state of Mayhem.

How do we deal with the fear involved in life? The first step on the road to the Top 1% is to learn to acknowledge fear and then proceed anyway. The vast majority of people will feel fear, allow it to take hold of them, and then turn away from whatever it is that's making them afraid. The elite performer recognizes that this fear is simply part of our primal nature and must be transcended as a prerequisite for accomplishment.

Top 1% performers understand that anxiety, complaining, and a victimhood mentality are often self-fulfilling prophecies driven by fear. Instead, transcendence of this fear through optimism and innovation is required. Animals do not have the ability to select their goals and create a vision for their lives. They are strictly focused on staying alive and procreating. We as humans, on the other hand, have something unique from animals, and that is *imagination*. We have the ability to create our lives based on the full use of our imagination, which can be used to reprogram our minds and recreate our images of ourselves.

EXERCISE: Top 1% ID Part II

To augment the previous questions from the Top 1% ID Part I, I want to add three more:

- What one thing do you think you are on earth for?
- What one thing would you focus on if nothing were impossible for you?
- What would you do differently if you knew you only had one year to live?

Once you get very clear on your own Top 1% ID, the goal is to build your life around these inspirational drivers in a conscious way. This is the best way to align your higher self and your primal self toward a common mission (we'll create your Major Mastery Mission together in Behavior #4, so stay with me). Making your core inspirational drivers very clear to your primal brain allows your primal brain to naturally pursue activities and opportunities that are highest on your personal hierarchy of inspirational drivers.

This is the foundation of personal growth, and this is how you'll optimize your higher self. This is obviously a skill that takes work to improve on, but it helps to build meaning into your life on a moment-to-moment basis as you deal with the fear, anxiety, and unhealthy desires that can otherwise be overwhelming. This is the beginning of the rest of your exciting journey of success and significance.

Chapter 4

BEHAVIOR #3:
CHOOSE LEADERSHIP AND MANAGE EGO

*Two different characters are presented to our emulation; the
one, of proud ambition and ostentatious avidity. The other, of
humble modesty and equitable justice. Two different models,
two different pictures, are held out to us, according to which
we may fashion our own character and behavior; the one
more gaudy and glittering in its colouring; the other more
correct and more exquisitely beautiful in its outline.*

~ Adam Smith ~

A s a Top 1% leader, it is your mission in life to live in such a way that when others see how you conduct yourself, they feel a stirring in their own souls to do more, be more, and shoulder a larger burden. Do that every single day of your life and you are making a conscious choice not only to serve yourself, but to serve others. This is the essence of Behavior #3: Choose Leadership and Manage Ego. Leadership comes in many different shapes and sizes, but the essence of leadership is moving others to positive action for a defined and specific purpose.

None of us sets out to be mediocre or live a life of little consequence. At some point along the way we give in to the idea that following the crowd and blending in is the safest thing to do. We do so because it causes the least amount of potential pain and discomfort for us. We find it easier to just blend in behind all our insecurities and weaknesses rather than stand out as unique and original.

We all live with certain insecurities and weaknesses, so the most common response to a call like mine to reach for the Top 1% is "I could never do that because I'm not good enough at anything to reach the elite level. That's for someone else." However, let me give you the hard evidence that this isn't true. It's what we've been conditioned to believe nonetheless.

As humans, we often cringe at the idea of change. We wait for chaos, tragedy, loss, bankruptcy, or even a devastating diagnosis before we decide to survey our behavior and feelings to make drastic change. For some reason we wait for the worst-case scenario to happen before we make an otherwise necessary shift.

In 2009, longtime palliative care nurse Bronnie Ware wrote a now famous blog post titled "Regrets of the Dying."[26] In the article she describes the top five most common themes that those she has cared for expressed to her at the end. She was typically by their side during

---

the last three to twelve weeks of their lives. When questioned about anything they would have done differently, the most common regret was: "I wish I'd had the courage to live a life true to myself, not the life others expected of me." In her own words, "When people realize that their life is almost over and look back clearly on it, it is easy to see how many dreams have gone unfulfilled."

Let that sink in for a moment. What this says to me is that most human beings spend their entire lives following the herd and doing what's "expected of them." They never make the decision to *choose leadership* and stand firm in their convictions. This is utterly heartbreaking.

Here's the cold hard truth: There is a veneer that serves as the outside covering for the real person underneath that you doubt others would like, accept, and admire. We are all so skilled at hiding our real selves that we often create a memorized set of automatic patterns to cover us up. We fabricate who we are to blend in more easily with the social, organizational, and even religious settings in which we find ourselves. This whole charade is based on deep insecurity and a lack of self-worth. And we all do it.

We are generally able to stay "busy" enough to keep the emotions associated with this masquerade under control. We get through school, establish our careers, get married, buy homes, and have children. Left unchecked, these external activities and achievements (or lack thereof) create our identities for us. This is not good, and it is the primary reason the term "mid-life crisis" exists. The sports cars, the affairs, and the plastic surgeries are all external ways of trying to further quiet the internal emotions we have never acknowledged. An empty desperation sets in that is so painful we'll do anything to divert our attention from it.

This is where addictions come from. The transient pleasure of a momentary shift of internal body chemistry drives this cycle forward.

Sadly, many of us follow the crowd into addiction (alcohol, drugs, pornography, television, and/or social media are the popular poisons of choice). Much of this is driven by the ego's profound desire to be liked, to gain prestige, and to "be somebody." It is the primal self wanting to display importance, overcome insecurity, and exert dominance.

The World Is in Leadership Crisis

So as human beings, where does this behavior lead us? In their Global Human Capital Trends 2014 report,[27] consulting firm Deloitte found the need for "leaders at all levels" to be one of the most critical issues companies face today, with 86% of those surveyed rating it as urgent or important. In fact, leaders from Deloitte wrote that cultivating leadership at every level "remains the No. 1 talent issue facing organizations around the world."

In the Old Testament book of 1 Kings, King David was preparing to pass from this life to the next around the year 970 BC. In doing so, he offered some final words to his son Solomon, who would eventually become known as the wisest man in the history of the world. King David's advice was telling: "I am about to go the way of all the earth. Be strong and show yourself a man" (1 Kings 2:2). In the Hebrew language, the words translated as "show yourself a man" mean something more like "become someone truly exceptional." By using these words, he was advising Solomon to demonstrate for others how to be exceptional by *being* a certain way himself. This is perhaps the best advice ever given. I intend to show you here the next step toward the Top 1% as it pertains to who *you* must be and what *you* must demonstrate to the world day in and day out.

Studies show that the strongest emotion present in a team of individuals radiates out and drives everyone on the team to resonate with

---

27 https://www2.deloitte.com/content/dam/Deloitte/ar/Documents/human-capital/
   arg_hc_global-human-capital-trends-2014_09062014%20(1).pdf.

that same emotion. But this process happens on a subconscious level, without anyone consciously knowing it is occurring. When the group gives attention to a strong negative emotion, and each member's mirror neurons (those nerve cells that allow us to mimic the behavior of others) begin to fire, the entire group spirals downward emotionally. As a leader, you have a huge impact on the emotion and psychology of your team and organization. Your team pays a lot of attention to you, your emotions, and your mannerisms. This is why most organizations are a mirror of the leader. Knowing this, it becomes even more important to consciously manage your own stress levels and emotional well-being.

The Leadership Misunderstanding

Understanding the current, highly flawed concept of "alpha" dominance is critical to your long-term success as a leader and an active participant in society. As a culture, we are obsessed with the "self-centered, push to get results" idea of what the alpha leader is meant to represent.

Even inside a wolf pack, there are so many more layers and levels than simple physical dominance and conflict. As an example, in the book *The Rise of Wolf 8*, author Rick McIntyre chronicles the movements of the famous Yellowstone wolf pack. He places a special focus on "Wolf 8," a nervous runt who was bullied by his bigger brothers yet grew up to become the alpha male of his pack. McIntyre recounts the courageous behavior of this young gray wolf facing up to a grizzly bear. He details how it affected the other members of the pack and their perception and treatment of him.

He explains that 8 rarely, if ever, challenged the other physically stronger members of the pack, and yet that lack of constant challenge, along with 8's ability to size up situations and respond in energetically economic ways, turned out to be key. His lack of constant dominance is the very behavior that set him up to be the one the pack chose to follow. Wolf 8 is a near-perfect example of the principles I espouse and teach my high-level coaching clients as part of the Shepherd Method of leadership through one-on-one coaching. Consistently courageous actions on behalf of the group carry much more weight than the meaningful displays of superiority or dominance by just one person.

Similarly, chimpanzees work their way up to alpha position by showing huge amounts of generosity with the group, displaying great interest and care for the infants and youngsters in the group, and of course by having great confidence in themselves. This comes at a price, as people, or in this case chimpanzees, are always coveting your position and want to bring you down.

So these alpha chimps are always watching their backs. This can lead to anxiety, insecurity, and potentially less confidence. The glucocorticoid level found in the bloodstream of alpha chimpanzees is just as high as the lowest-ranking chimpanzee in the group. Basically, everyone else in between has a much lower stress level and lower levels of glucocorticoids, along with a more robust immune system. This goes to show that less stress will almost always create a healthier lifestyle.

Science has shown that the smallest chimpanzee in a group can still be the alpha male. Size actually has very little to do with who the alpha is. Something called the coalition system shows how male chimpanzees who make the "right" social connections by choosing their coalition partners carefully are most likely to find themselves in alpha roles. So, you may be asking, "What does this mean for me?"

The Next Generation of Leadership

There is perhaps nothing less effective yet more tolerated (and in some cases celebrated) than the egomaniac in a position of authority. The egomaniac sees everything from the perspective of themselves as the center of the universe. This creates an inability to acknowledge and learn from mistakes, makes enemies, and oddly enough feeds insecurity. This is often because the egotistical position of being driven by the primal self makes flaws and weaknesses fundamental to the egomaniac's personal identity.

Of course, there's also the issue of imposter syndrome, the feeling of anxiety and discomfort associated with not feeling deserving of the success you've had with the position you hold. This is a fabricated byproduct of insecurity in your own mind, but it is one of the other dangers of an ego-driven approach.

Alternatively, authentic Shepherd Leaders understand their strengths and weaknesses, which brings an inner peace and clarity of mind that is so crucial. You must be characterized by making the decision to set your own Top 1% standards, knowing when to ignore the opinions of others and the need to continually prove yourself. You recognize your inherent flaws, but they're not central to your personal identity, so you have no need to cover-up for them.

General Colin Powell once advised, "Avoid having your ego so close to your position that when your position falls, your ego goes with it."

This concept of the Alpha 1.0, which is often grounded in ego-based leadership, is extremely harmful to the development of key leaders and their teams. That leads us to wonder: What else is available to leaders? How else can leaders lead? The answer lies in the fundamental underpinnings of Shepherd Leadership philosophies and the key differences between the Alpha 1.0 and Shepherd Leadership. The Alpha 1.0 disciple allows others to define his identity and self-worth. He is desperate for tribal validation. He's handcuffed by how he thinks he should look, how he should act, and how he should be. But there's a paradox here that is very sad. The Alpha 1.0 is so ego-driven and self-obsessed that he has a very hard time taking any definitive independent action toward his meaningful goals and unique mission. He fears becoming the most authentic version of himself, so he remains inauthentic and without access to a higher form of energy that only comes from spiritual connection (see Behavior #7).

Due to his insecurity, it is difficult for him to acknowledge and take responsibility for his mistakes. He feels that acknowledging a mistake and apologizing would be a sign of weakness or "being soft," which could be taken advantage of by others. A byproduct of this sad truth is that the Alpha 1.0 is insensitive, self-loathing, and lacking in compassion because he knows in his heart he has turned away from his higher self (see Behavior #2). Sadly, there are many Alpha 1.0s walking around the boardrooms and residing in the corner offices of high-powered businesses. Their leadership style, and the ultimate

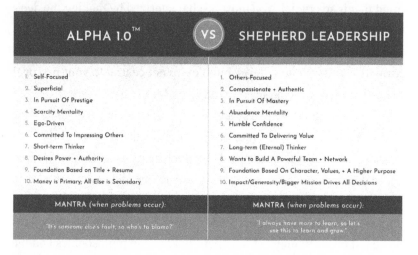

ALPHA 1.0™	VS	SHEPHERD LEADERSHIP
1. Self-Focused		1. Others-Focused
2. Superficial		2. Compassionate + Authentic
3. In Pursuit Of Prestige		3. In Pursuit Of Mastery
4. Scarcity Mentality		4. Abundance Mentality
5. Ego-Driven		5. Humble Confidence
6. Committed To Impressing Others		6. Committed To Delivering Value
7. Short-term Thinker		7. Long-term (Eternal) Thinker
8. Desires Power + Authority		8. Wants to Build A Powerful Team + Network
9. Foundation Based on Title + Resume		9. Foundation Based On Character, Values, + A Higher Purpose
10. Money is Primary; All Else is Secondary		10. Impact/Generosity/Bigger Mission Drives All Decisions
MANTRA (when problems occur):		MANTRA (when problems occur):
"It's someone else's fault, so who's to blame?"		"I always have more to learn, so let's use this to learn and grow."

impact of their decisions, trickles down throughout the entire organization. Alpha 1.0s don't serve the best interests of their teams and organizations; they serve their own selfish interests.

Here is the truth you must come to grips with: The "group" isn't thinking about you at all. Frankly, they don't give a damn. The best thing you can do is become a Shepherd Leader so you can be the role model they need and guide them through their pain. We do this through shifting our leadership tendencies and behaviors outward or developing into a Shepherd Leader.

The Shepherd Leader is compassionate, authentic, others-focused, and in constant pursuit of Mastery. He is guided by a foundation based on character, values, and a higher purpose. He acknowledges his mistakes, looks for learning opportunities, and apologizes with sincerity when he knows he's failed to be his best. He thinks with an eternal perspective, acts with humble confidence, and knows that without a deep connection with a higher power he is infinitely limited. He has also taken the time to deeply search for his unique calling, which I refer to as his Major Mastery Mission. (You'll be creating yours as you adopt Behavior #4: Commit to Mastery.)

The Four Hallmarks of Shepherd Leadership

1. Self-Confidence (vs. Insecurity)
2. Solution-Orientation (all problems are solvable)
3. Service-Orientation (vs. Self-Focus)
4. Attitude of Autonomy (vs. Entitlement)

Shepherd Leaders are characterized by a healthy level of self-confidence because they've earned the respect and admiration of others and feel worthy.

They display solution-orientation through an attitude that they can address and solve all problems in their path. Shepherd Leaders also have a growth mindset and believe in a future free of limitations, recognizing they can constantly acquire new skills along their journey.

They demonstrate service-orientation by being concerned with the well-being and care of others, rather than solely themselves. This orientation comes from an abundance mindset in which one sees the world as having more than adequate resources for everyone. Life is not about taking what's yours before someone else takes it. Instead, it's about enhancing the success and growth of others as you pursue your own growth and success. The logical outworking of this abundance philosophy is an attitude of generosity—a genuine desire for others to have what you have and to experience all the joys you experience. It's also a clear recognition of the duty of a steward, because whatever resources we may enjoy in this life are not truly "ours" anyway.

Finally, Shepherd Leaders maintain an attitude of autonomy. This is characterized by absolute certainty of their unique Top 1% ID and pursuit of their Major Mastery Mission. This is what allows the Shepherd Leader to resist the temptation to adopt a herd mentality or compare him or herself to others. This attitude of autonomy is a crucial defining characteristic and the one we will focus on moving forward.

An Attitude of Autonomy

As Theodore Roosevelt once said, "Comparison is the thief of joy." If you truly want to impact others and reach the top, you must stop comparing yourself to them. Far too often we look at other people and make their approval the standard we feel obligated to meet. As a consequence, we waste our own limitless potential and never pursue our Major Mastery Mission. Instead, Behavior #3 calls you to *choose leadership* by determining the path of your own life. In the words of Victor Frankl, "Everyone has his own specific vocation or Mission in life…Therein he cannot be replaced, nor can his life be repeated. Thus, everyone's task is as unique as his specific opportunity to implement it."

Pro-Tip: Visual Triggers for How to Be

Set up visual triggers to remind yourself "how to be" in every given role you have. This can be a sticky note on the dashboard of your vehicle, a note in your journal, or even an alarm set on your phone to remind you throughout the day how to show up. What are the behaviors and traits you want to have as a parent? As a boss? As an employee? As a son or daughter? As a friend? If you don't make these notes in a visible place you will not perform at your best. Be intentional about this.

Later in his career, psychologist Abraham Maslow studied a group of individuals he termed *transcenders*, finding that this group of people were able to see connections between seemingly unrelated ideas, making them better innovators. He also found that transcending scientists "showed humility, a sense of ignorance, a feeling of smallness, all before the tremendousness of the universe."[28]

A lot of your fears around failure and lack of self-worth are related to poor inherent values. You already know my stance regarding the choices you and I make. The choices you make in every area of life (including the values you hold dear and whether you've explored your own inspirational drivers) are 100% your responsibility. Embracing this philosophy is Behavior #1. If we agree that leadership is a choice, then it should be held as a high value for anyone aspiring to reach the Top 1%. And clearly that includes you. When you place leadership high on your value hierarchy, you filter the other choices you make in life based on that leadership value. This brings huge amounts of clarity to your decision making.

For example, as a leader, if a core value is ensuring everyone you encounter likes you, you're setting yourself up for insecurity and self-worth issues because you're placing the power of the outcome outside of yourself and in the hands of others. This is a recipe for disaster and pain. Note that wanting everyone to like you is not an inherently bad desire. But you can't set this up as one of your values if you wish to live a life of autonomy, success, and confidence. There are simply too many non-controllable variables.

A better example of a value you may want to incorporate in your own life that I'll discuss in a future behavior is building a strong net-

---

28 Maslow, A.H. *The Farther Reaches of Human Nature*, New York: Viking press, 1971, p. 290.

work of meaningful relationships. This is within your realm of ability to influence through your efforts to choose worthwhile individuals in which to invest relationship equity.

The way the soul ties back to leadership is that leaders define the life they're going to lead by creating a foundational structure of worthwhile values and inspirational drivers that is unique to them. This is a choice, and it's why you must *choose leadership*. As you live your inspirational drivers, your personal sense of integrity, control, inner peace, and potential for growth will boost your energy exponentially. You'll begin to respect yourself more and compare yourself to others much less.

The Performance Principle

The performance principle states that your worth as a person is predicated on your ability to accomplish great things and achieve at a high level. I take achievement seriously, and it's one of my strongest personal drivers. But the danger here is that this is a ridiculously incomplete view of life. This is the epitome of Alpha 1.0 at work. Most of the greatest principles in life are paradoxical. For example, until you're able to find inherent self-worth you'll never have authentic confidence in yourself, your abilities, and your own value. Once you get beyond this performance principle as the only standard, you're able to achieve the most important things in your life based on your inspirational drivers much more easily without all the unneeded pulling and tugging of expectation, guilt, and pain associated with whatever you think is the role you're "supposed" to play.

There's a continuous temptation to *have* instead of to *be*. In other words, we tend to care a little bit more about what positions we have, or what status we have, rather than who we are as individuals and the depth of our character. We get caught up in chasing status and recognition rather than virtue. I have nothing against recognition or status. But the order in which we place these priorities is the crucial distinction. Virtue must come first. To have more, you must first become more.

Researchers have recently discovered that new genes in your central nervous system turn themselves on ONLY when you place yourself in new situations (more on this as we move further toward personal mastery). When the genes are turned on, they code for proteins that serve to build new structures in your brain. This means that much of you is literally *yet to be created*. But, in order to improve and evolve, you must *choose leadership* by willingly placing yourself in situations that require you to level up.

Putting yourself in these types of scenarios literally "builds" your character. By taking on new challenges and performing well, you *become* a person who performs at a high level when taking on challenges. If, however, you shrink back into avoidance or simply follow the crowd, you *become* a coward destined for mediocrity (or worse). If you allow yourself to be inauthentic, dishonest, or irresponsible, you weaken your character. With a weak character you will degenerate into the type of person who does awful things—or at the very least allows awful things—and any type of hardship will ruin you.

I want to make it clear that your performance and posture toward life matter a great deal. People at the top reap rewards that those in the middle and bottom aren't privy to. NOT EVERYONE GETS A TROPHY. In fact, most don't. Not only do the mediocre and substandard performers NOT get rewards, they get sick, depressed, addicted, and disenchanted. The most predictable way to the Top 1% is to choose to become a Shepherd Leader.

The Big Questions

As humans we tend to lean toward oppositional energy. We base our identity on the disdain for or even the pity of a common enemy. If you're Catholic, it's "Oh those poor Protestants, I'm so glad we're not like them." What a waste! This is also the basis of bigotry and racism. Being driven by this kind of thinking is a clear sign you're not choosing leadership.

This is precisely why you must *choose leadership and manage ego.* This is the time to ask the big questions. What is my purpose in life? Is there a God? What is success? And my personal favorite: What must I achieve in life so that when I look back in the last few moments on earth, I will view my life as successful? When you take the time to ask these questions, you realize nothing in your external environment will ever repair who you are internally. Eventually you come to understand it is futile to try to maintain some specific persona to make others happy. You must choose the inner contentment that comes from answering the deep questions for yourself and building your life around the answers. That's what leaders do, and you *choose leadership and manage ego.*

If the image you display to the outer world is not consistent with the real you that answers these questions in an honest and meaningful way, then the amount of energy you'll expend to maintain the artificial image will be devastating and debilitating. It's an unsustainable way to live a life of purpose and impact. When you pretend to like things you resent, or you stay silent when you know you should speak up, your ego has taken over (our old friend the primal self) and devastation and desperation are close behind. But when you live a life of authentic transparency externally consistent with your internal inspirational drivers, this previously expended energy is freed up to help you design the reality and life you desire.

The Archetype

The archetypal example of Shepherd Leadership, of course, is Jesus Christ. Whether you are Christian or not, the historical person of

Christ is one ideal example of the acceptance of radical responsibility, choosing leadership, and management of ego. In sharp contrast to Shepherd Leadership, there is Satan. He personifies arrogant power, deception, and refusal of sacrifice. The temptation of Christ by Satan in the Gospel of Luke (chapter 4) is the ideal display of the Good Shepherd overcoming the inherent chaos and tyranny of the world personified by Satan. Satan tempted Jesus to turn a stone into bread to satisfy His hunger, to worship Satan for the promise of earthly authority and fame, and to test God by displaying His own power. The lesson I want you to take from this account is how leadership truly does start with the self. You earn the privilege of leading others by leading *yourself* well first. And if Jesus made it a high priority to humble Himself and refuse His own ego, perhaps you and I should take notice and consider it as well.

Three Categories of People

There are only three fundamental categories of people—*avoiders, blind followers,* and *Shepherd Leaders.* Blind followers and avoiders collectively make up the Alpha 1.0 tribe and encompass 99% of us walking on this earth. Each of these categories has a different approach toward life, neither one effective. Avoiders have an overt lack of maturity and no personal autonomy—they don't "choose leadership." Blind followers are driven entirely by ego in the form of a desire for social approval and an increased position in the social hierarchy—they can't "manage ego." Shepherd Leaders both choose leadership and manage ego.

Avoiders have not progressed past a childish attitude toward life. All their decisions in life boil down to seeking pleasure and avoiding pain. It's really no more complex than that. Avoiders are easily influenced, and they are content to be influenced by the promise of more pleasure and less pain. Avoiders are choosing to not actively participate in the game. A large number of "leaders" fall into this category. This is not the category for you.

In contrast, but only slightly better, are the blind followers. Blind followers are slightly more advanced than avoiders. The key with this group is that they base their decisions and identity on social feedback and social roles. Nothing is done for its inherent value or virtue, but rather for some calculated transaction through which they can gain an advantage. Blind followers are obsessed with what other people think of them, how popular they are, and where they can gain ground on the social hierarchy.

These folks are often quite charming and charismatic, but their motives are counterfeit. Many powerful politicians, elected officials, and highly influential socialites fall into this category. The real weakness with this group is that they stand for nothing. And as they say, "If you stand for nothing, you'll fall for anything." You can't live a life of leadership and meaning this way because you're not living your own life based on your unique inspirational drivers.

But then there is the third group, the Shepherd Leaders. This group has come to understand and embrace the realization that the most meaningful and significant things in life have value for their own sakes, apart from any external validation, social approval, or material gain. Honesty, integrity, generosity, contribution, service, hard work, and humility are key guiding principles for the Shepherd Leader because they are inherently right and good. Shepherd Leaders are always humble and kind but never compromise on their convictions. You are called to be a Shepherd Leader.

An important thing to realize about these three categories is that they are age and position independent. High school students can be Shepherd Leaders, and seasoned professionals and entrepreneurs can be blind followers. The differentiator is in the way you do things and the "why" behind what you do. Shepherd Leaders are the people who hold the world together. These are the leaders who take the fall for their team's mistakes, the friends who hold us accountable and make us better, and the parents who sacrifice their own comfort for the best interest of their children. The way in which Shepherd Leaders conduct themselves is laid out for you in great detail throughout this book. Carefully study and adopt these seven behaviors and you will put yourself in this category. I won't dare to say it's *easy*, but it is as *simple* as that.

The Case for Humility

You might think that humility as a virtue is little more than a quaint idea from yesteryear, but that is not the case. In fact, it is a vital component of Shepherd Leadership and Top 1% performance. Science reveals how humility is centered on accurately knowing your own strengths and weaknesses, as well as recognizing there is a much bigger context to consider beyond yourself. Having this broader perspective and the freedom that comes with it is essential. The Shepherd Leader recognizes his abilities and asks how he can contribute; he recognizes his flaws and asks how he can grow.

A 2016 Duke University study of 155 individuals[29] split the participants into two groups based on having intellectual humility or intellectual arrogance. The intellectually humble group admitted their answers were likely not always right and that their views could be changed when confronted with new information. The intellectually arrogant group took the position that they were rarely wrong and never changed their minds.

The first task was to read a list of forty statements on a range of controversial topics—military drone strikes, common core curricula in schools, same-sex marriage, and more. Then they took a survey

29 Deffler, S., Leary, M. R., & Hoyle, R. H. Knowing What You Know: Intellectual Humility and Judgments of Recognition Memory. *Personality and Individual Differences*, 96, 2016, pp. 255-259.

to measure how familiar they were with all kinds of random topics (Susan B. Anthony, Mount Rushmore, and so on). But there was a catch in that a third of the topics were bogus, such as a fictitious "Hamrick's Rebellion."

Finally, participants read another list of sixty statements in order to determine which statements were on the first list and which were new, along with their level of confidence in each decision. The intellectually humble took longer to read the first controversial statements—especially if the information ran counter to their beliefs. They were better at identifying new statements, and, when wrong, they had a sense they were making a mistake.

By contrast, the intellectually arrogant only skimmed through the reading, were less accurate at identifying statements as new, and were sure their wrong responses were correct. They were also more susceptible to the fake news items, meaning they didn't know what they didn't know. The contrast between humility and arrogance couldn't be clearer:

> ...researchers observed that the intellectually humble have a constant desire to learn and improve. They embrace ambiguity and the unknown. They like getting new information. They even enjoy finding out when they're wrong. And when in trouble, they're more willing to accept help. Humble college students have been found to be higher in academic achievement. They improved more over the course of a semester, and they got better grades. The intellectually arrogant are convinced they have the right answers, certain they've heard it all before. They're even threatened by new information. They perceive new facts not as facts, but as a passive-aggressive statement that you think they're ignorant.[30]

---

30 See https://www.washingtonpost.com/news/inspired-life/wp/2016/12/08/leaders-are-more-powerful-when-theyre-humble-new-research-shows.

Bradley Owens and David Hekman have studied humble leaders in a wide range of organizational contexts and reached a number of important conclusions about humility in leadership:[31]

- Humble leaders prioritize organizational success over their own success.
- Companies led by humble CEOs have less pay disparity from top to bottom.
- They disperse their power, hire more diverse managers, and empower staff to lead and innovate.
- Companies with a humble CEO have less turnover, better employee satisfaction, and higher overall performance.
- Humble leaders admit mistakes and recognize their own limitations.
- A humble leader doesn't assume success is inevitable and is therefore driven to improve.
- The humble leader doesn't have all the answers and solicits feedback.
- Humble leaders celebrate the successes of others more than their own.
- Humble leaders don't have less authority but have greater flexibility in how they use their power, saving it for when it's really needed and otherwise being more participatory.
- Followers of humble leaders are more motivated and work harder because they know the leader is counting on them to step up.
- The humble leader is willing to revise plans and strategies based on new information.
- Both humility and arrogance can be "caught and taught" because they're "contagious."

---

31 Owens, B. and Hekman, D. How does leader humility influence team performance? Exploring the Mechanisms of Contagion and Collective Promotion Focus, *Academy of Management Journal*, 59(3), 2015.

Here's how Owens and Hekman sum it all up: "Our findings suggest that humility appears to embolden individuals to aspire to their highest potential and enables them to make the incremental improvements necessary to progress toward that potential." To that end, effective and meaningful leaders often lead with humility. They don't make it about themselves; it is courageously about others. Make no mistake, humility works!

Make the Decision

Make the decision to *not keep up* with a culture of failed leadership. It is not the actual knowledge of inferiority in your ability or skills that hinders your performance. It is the sensation or feelings of inferiority or inadequacy that causes you the trouble. We often bring this on ourselves through our constant tendency to judge ourselves not against our own standard, but against some other person's norm. This is a losing proposition because by default you will choose to compare yourself to someone who is slightly ahead of you in some particular way. You will stack the cards against yourself from the beginning, which will make you feel miserable and inferior. *Choosing leadership* is about guiding yourself and your organization in a progressive manner and controlling the controllables, independent of someone else's yardstick. Your objective should not be to feel superior or inferior to others, but rather to continually commit to the improvement and development of your own unique characteristics and accomplishments as well as those of your organization.

The first move toward *choosing leadership and refusing ego* is always introspective, learning who you really are and connecting with those inspirational drivers. Know this with real clarity and everything else will gradually fall into place. We were all born unique, and this uniqueness is marked genetically in our DNA. In fact, your genetic makeup has never occurred before and will never be repeated again. God designed you this way. Your foundational mission in this life is also unique and will never be exactly repeated. That's also the way God designed it.

You're born with this uniqueness, but part of your life journey is to bring that uniqueness out into the world through your work and contribution. What weakens this inner burning desire and creates doubt is the herd mentality and the social pressure to fall in line and conform. People may think you're bizarre, but that's the price you have to pay. You cannot allow yourself to become a follower if you hope to reach the Top 1%. You must trust your unique calling. You absolutely must *choose leadership*.

The road to the Top 1% begins when you discover who you are. The emphasis I'm placing on developing your inspirational drivers and uniqueness might seem a bit whimsical, but it's actually very practical. We're moving into a world with much less security from corporations, the government, or friends and family that will protect us. The world is competitive, and you must rise to the occasion to the utmost of your ability.

Intense Intentionality

Choosing leadership requires you to maintain an intense intentionality about where to focus your energy and to protect that focus from outside distractions. This includes trivial decisions like deciding what type of clothes to wear and what to eat. It is important to remove things from your life that unnecessarily drain your energy. You'll have to begin saying no to a lot of things that you might otherwise allow in. That gives you the space and ability to say yes when those rare opportunities present themselves that are a good use of your engagement and energy.

Experiments[32] show that people who were forced to make choices among a range of multiple different consumer goods, such as T-shirt

32   Vohs, Kathleen; Baumeister, Roy; Twenge, Jean; Schmeichel, Brandon; Tice, Dianne; Crocker, Jennifer (2005). "Decision Fatigue Exhausts Self-Regulatory Resources — But So Does Accommodating to Unchosen Alternatives"

colors, types of candy, and types of shampoo, actually performed worse than those presented with only one option on tests of everything from physical stamina to persistence to problem solving. The conclusion of the research was that even when it comes to the simplest of things, making multiple decisions can leave a person deprived of the energy it takes to perform at a high level.

The key habit for maximizing mental energy is to make a routine out of just about everything that is not essential to your mission. When you make decisions on an automatic basis you conserve mental muscle. Interestingly, Albert Einstein, Mark Zuckerberg, Steve Jobs, and even President Barack Obama practiced eliminating trivial decisions such as what clothes to wear and what foods to eat for higher performance.

Pro-Tip: Automatize Trivial Decisions

Here are some key tips to automatize trivial decisions for higher performance:

- *Think about all the decisions you make in a typical day and automate as many of them as possible that don't really matter. Examples might include what clothing to wear, what to eat at mealtime, when to go to the gym, and what events to say yes or no to attending.*
- *Never spend energy on gossip or worrying what others think of you (they're likely not thinking about you anyway).*
- *Stop watching the news (it drains your energy and causes needless anxiety; if something important happens someone in your life will tell you).*

Always be humble and kind, but never compromise your convictions. *Choose leadership and manage ego.*

Chapter 5

BEHAVIOR #4:
STRATEGICALLY DESIGN YOUR REALITY

*Aren't you in awe when you contemplate the mysteries of
Eternity, of life, of the marvelous structure behind reality?
And this is the miracle of the human mind—to use its
constructions, concepts, and formulas as tools to explain
what man sees, feels, and touches. Try to comprehend
a little more each day. Have holy curiosity.*

~ Albert Einstein ~

A s we shift our leadership methods and style from one centered on the self (the ego) to one centered on the better good of all (the team), we can also begin to better design our reality to one that serves our highest interests. It's within our nature as human beings to view our current circumstances as incomplete and the future as infinitely better. The "grass is always greener" attitude is one we often struggle with. Even so, perhaps this is a God-given mechanism built in to get us to take some freaking action. I'm not certain, but it's effective nonetheless. You have the ability to see in your mind's eye exactly the future you wish to bring about. We must employ this gift with precision and persistence to reach the Top 1%. Remember, your current situation is just a temporary take on your reality. You can always change it.

Pulling Back the Curtain

We all perceive that we live in a certain "reality." But have you ever considered how we create that reality? In Behavior #1, I encouraged you to embrace radical responsibility so that you use your limitless amount of unfocused potential energy. In that behavior you made the decision to draw the line in the sand and shoulder the burden of your own circumstances. In this behavior, strategically designing your reality, you will start to use your imagination and creativity to create your ideal life in your mind's eye. Doing so will bring it into your physical reality.

If you're a very literal person, you might come to this section with a healthy dose of skepticism about the role visualization plays in your success and achievement. And in many ways you're right. Visualization alone, with no action, does nothing to create success. However, research out of Oxford and Cambridge suggests that your ability to vividly imagine details about a specific future dramatically increases your energy and momentum. This leads to constructive action. When your mind's eye can picture exactly what the future looks like, it can point you in the direction of the future you imagine.[33]

It will be helpful to start here by looking at your past. But I only want you to look at a few valuable things from your past. First look at all the situations where you confronted risk and acted with courage, with no guarantee that you would be successful. Next, look at all the new skills and capabilities you've acquired in the past that seemed impossible to you at one point in time. This glimpse into the past will show you that despite your often limited thinking, you have the capacity to create the future reality you desire.

The World You See

Your understanding of the world means a great deal to your overall progress and success. For example, the clearer the picture you can get in your mind of the way the world works in both the seen and unseen realms, the more you'll be able to use that understanding to design the reality you want. You've no doubt heard that your thoughts and choices create your life. It's also true that you create the contents of your mind by dictating the things you expose it to. This includes your environment, such as the books you read, the courses you take and implement, and the people you surround yourself with. You are now comfortable with the idea of embracing radical responsibility in your life, so you know your environment and the way you nurture your own mind is entirely on you. You are in charge of who you're becoming, so you must strategically design your reality.

---

33   Holmes. E.A., James, E.L., Blackwell, S.E., and Hales, S. They flash upon that inward eye, *The Psychologist*, May 2011, volume 24, pp. 340-343. Available online at https://thepsychologist.bps.org.uk/volume-24/edition-5/they-flash-upon-inward-eye.

Pro-Tip: Energy Transmutation

1. *Become consciously aware of your negative emotional reactions (fear, anger, shame, envy, lust).*
2. *Shift that negative emotional energy into its positive correlating emotion (fear to courage, anger to commitment, envy to admiration, lust to ambition).*
3. *Focus on the new positive emotion with self-talk that supports the new emotion and holds the old negative emotion back from resurfacing.*
4. *Take action using the new emotion.*

Scientists have discovered many laws that govern the operation of what we perceive as the physical world. The application of these physical laws over the last few centuries has literally molded the progression of civilization.

In classical Newtonian physics, all things were considered solid. For example, energy was explained as a force to change the physical state of matter in some way. But as you'll learn, energy is far more than some "force" exerted on material things. Energy is the very essence of all existence.

Albert Einstein's famous equation $E=MC^2$ demonstrated that energy and matter are essentially one and the same thing. Energy and matter are interchangeable. This was a huge revelation at the time. The point is that we have an overly simplistic and very limited understanding of the concepts of energy and matter, as well as our role in transforming one into the other.

More Than Meets the Eye: Double-Slit Experiments

In the early twentieth century, physicists witnessed the emergence of a multitude of seemingly counterintuitive discoveries that challenged the idea of material reality being the only reality. The gap physicists discovered in their understanding of matter and energy made way for the field we now know as *quantum physics.*

Specifically, in the 1920s, scientists discovered that light can behave as either a particle or a wave. This concept is described as the *dual-behavior of matter.* An even more mind-blowing discovery was that light or matter only behaves like particles in the presence of what scientists term an *intelligent observer.* Let me explain further.

There are a series of repeatable experiments known as *double-slit experiments.* In these experiments, scientists demonstrate the wavelike nature of light by shining a single light beam through two side-by-side vertical slits or openings in a barrier. This creates two new and separate side-by-side beams of light. These two new beams of light interfere with each other just like waves in a body of water would come into contact with one another and cause interference. Think about it like this—when two bodies of water come together, they form a larger body of water. Two troughs create a deeper trough. When crests of water come together, they form a higher crest. But when troughs and crests meet, they cancel one another out based on their respective depths and heights.

To better understand the full nature of light, physicists then came up with another type of double-slit experiment. Rather than shining a light continuously through the slits, they came up with a way to send one photon of light at a time through the slits. Since photons are the particle version of light, the scientists expected to notice a pattern form on the detector similar to the pattern bullets might make when fired from a gun into a target. Shockingly, though, even as only one photon was released at a time, each individual photon still behaved as if it were part of a wave interfering with another wave. This type of behavior doesn't seem likely or even possible, yet they confirmed this by repeating the experiments.

Trying to understand how this inexplicable result could occur, physicists then conducted another experiment using a measuring device to detect which slit an individual photon actually traveled through. The measuring device does NOT interfere in any way with the passage of the photons through the slits. Once they added the measuring device to the experiment, the photons again passed through the slits and hit the detector like fired bullets. Literally, the only difference in the two experimental setups was that the passage of the photons through the slits had been measured by an "intelligent observer" in the second experiment. Since then, physicists have gone on to prove thousands of times that until measured by an intelligent observer, everything—whether energy such as light or matter such as atoms—behaves in a wavelike manner until measured by an intelligent observer. The important conclusion is this: *An intelligent observer plays a key role in the actual formation of matter as we know it.*

It gets more interesting. In 1976, a British stomach cancer group conducted a randomized, controlled study of a potential chemotherapy treatment for stomach cancer. The results of the study, published in May 1983 in *The World Journal of Surgery*,[34] reported on 411 patients that took part in the double-blind study. Neither the patients nor the clinicians knew who received a placebo saline treatment and who received the actual chemotherapy drug treatment. The study lasted for several months, and ultimately *30% of the patients who were given the saline drip lost all their hair!* People who thought they were receiving chemotherapy lost their hair because that's what they expected would happen.

These experiments show that physical reality is created only when intelligent observers (you and I) are present to convert wavelike energy into particulate matter through focused observation. The

---

34   See https://link.springer.com/article/10.1007/BF01658089.

physical reality you and I experience is both created and altered nearly exclusively by our focused thinking (thought energy).

Our Senses Are Limited: Newtonian vs. Quantum Atoms

It is obvious that matter is nothing like what our senses tell us it is. In fact, the majority of reality is hidden from our senses. For example, our eyes detect only visible light, which is a tiny portion of the electromagnetic spectrum that includes radio waves, ultraviolet rays, X-rays, microwaves, and gamma waves, none of which can be perceived through our sense of sight. If we could actually see the rest of the spectrum, we would perceive the world entirely made of light.

As far as hearing goes, we can only detect sound vibrating in the 20–20,000 Hz range, but sounds can vibrate in frequency well beyond 20,000 Hz (like atoms, for example, which vibrate at 10 trillion HZ). As for the lower range of sound, things like earthquakes, volcanoes, and lightning all vibrate as slowly as 0.001 Hz. Our senses of taste, smell, and touch are similarly limited. It's fair to say our senses can't detect 99.9% of the wavelengths, frequencies, and vibrating substances around us at all times. This is actually confirmation that matter is an illusion made of vibrating energy.

The diagram of an atom we all saw in school shows the nucleus made up of protons and neutrons surrounded by circling electrons. But that is a very distorted picture of what we now know to be true at the subatomic level. The hydrogen atom is the most common atom teachers show us because it's the simplest. The first issue we run into is that to be in proper scale, the electron would have to be drawn several miles away from the nucleus. In actuality, if all the space between the nucleus of the atom and the orbiting electrons was removed, our physical bodies would be less than the size of the head of a pin. As mind-blowing as it is, our bodies consist almost entirely of empty space. The second major misunderstanding is that we perceive of the atom diagram as static.

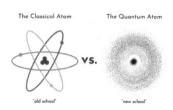

The Classical Atom   The Quantum Atom

vs.

'old school'   'new school'

In reality, the electron pictured as a dot in a circle around the nucleus is actually moving at the speed of light. A single electron will circle the nucleus of an atom trillions of times in just one second! Moving at the speed of light, the electron basically creates a shell of light energy around the nucleus. In fact, larger atoms create what's described as an "electron cloud" around the nucleus. It's this electron cloud, almost like a force field, that keeps our mostly space-filled body from sinking into the ground or collapsing. Oh, and by the way, the nucleus isn't made of matter either. Protons and neutrons are also composed of energy moving at the speed of light. Einstein made this point in 1905 in his paper describing his special theory of relativity, in which he made the claim that the nucleus of an atom is actually a super-condensed, high-frequency form of energy. The absence of any solid matter at the core of the atom has been proven over and over in particle accelerator experiments.

Everything Is Energy

This idea that matter is only energy in a vibrating equilibrium is known as *quantum field theory*. This is the act of describing fields at the subatomic level. Everything we perceive—from the world around us that seems so solid to the very sensation of weight—is energy interacting with energy. The fact that matter results from the invisible organization of energy hints that it may be possible, even likely, that this invisible organization can be altered. *Matter is not fixed but changeable, and we can change it.*

Current understandings in physics, quantum theory, and string theory place the physical universe as a small three-dimensional energy bubble in a virtually infinite two-dimensional sea of energy, referred to as the *energy-verse*. What's the evidence for this?

When Einstein was developing his theory of general relativity, he struggled to understand why gravity's combined strength throughout the universe isn't causing the universe to contract. To get his equations to match up to reality, Einstein created the idea of the cosmological constant, the constant level of undetected background energy present in the universe that pushes against the force of gravity created by matter. The problem with the original mathematical value he chose for the cosmological constant was that when he inserted it into his equations, it maintained the universe in a static state.

The trouble was, Edwin Hubble showed that the universe is in fact expanding. This discovery caused Einstein to call the idea of the cosmological constant his "greatest blunder." Either way, the idea that the universe contains more energy than can be currently measured remains a requirement in general relativity equations. Otherwise the equations don't match up to the measured behavior of the universe.

Here's where quantum physics comes in. Quantum physicists believe the background energy exists in a quantum energy field commonly referred to as the "quantum field," which is believed to be equal in potency at every point in the universe. This quantum energy field is thought to be quite active, and theoretical physicist John Archibald Wheeler at Princeton described this ceaseless activity as "quantum foam."

String Theory

Further research into the accelerating expansion of the universe discovered that the entirety of matter in the known universe only accounts for about 5% of the gravity! So what accounts for the remaining 95%? Enter string theory.

String theory suggests that everything rises from a two-dimensional ocean of small rings and strings of vibrating energy that forms everything including space itself. But what leads to the idea of string theory? Well, the answer has to do with math. The actual math isn't important, but the concept behind it is. String theory is an attempt to solve the mystery of the incompatibility of the mathematical systems of general relativity and quantum theory. Having these two branches in physics be mathematically incoherent is like having two major languages be untranslatable to one another. The major discrepancy between relativity and quantum theory (which string theory resolves) is in calculating how much energy actually exists in space.

M-theory, specifically, is string theory's most accepted version and posits that the higher energy predicted by quantum theory *does actually exist somewhere else*. M-theory's stance is that the energy exists in extra dimensions beyond the four dimensions general relativity concerns itself with. Those dimensions are the three dimensions of space and one of time. Those extra dimensions exist beyond our senses and beyond the ability of our current best technology to detect. In M-theory, the three dimensions of our already almost impossibly large physical universe are the smallest dimensions that exist in the cosmos!

Now here's where it gets exciting. Although these high-frequency energies are not perceptible by our senses or our most sensitive instruments, they interpenetrate our universe at every point. Although our little bubble of a universe is three-dimensionally self-contained (meaning we can't travel outside of it or see outside of it), these two-dimensional energies fill it and interpenetrate it like water does a sponge. Even though the frequency of these energies is so high and the wavelengths so small that they're undetectable by us, string theorists and quantum physicists are positive that if these energies were not present, the universe would simply disappear. This energy-verse that interpenetrates our universe is what Heisenberg labeled the realm of potential, and it is the ocean of energy rings and strings from which all matter and space originally formed. The essential qualities of the energy-verse are that it exists beyond the physical universe, it is nearly infinite, and it contains only immaterial high-frequency vibrating energy.

So What?

Here's why it all matters: the energy-verse invisibly penetrates the physical universe at every point. To that end, we simultaneously exist in both the physical realm and the energy-verse. And like the universe, our physical body is interpenetrated by the invisible energy of the energy-verse. Though we can't perceive the interpenetrating energy with our senses, we are all aware of it to a certain degree. It's what gives us excitement, joy, or sometimes nervous energy associated with anxiety. It causes you to have a rush of adrenaline, a dragged-down feeling of depression, or chronic fatigue. It's also called the *life-force* that keeps your heart pumping, your body digesting, your lungs breathing, and your more than fifty trillion cells in working order moment-to-moment.

The conventional model considers the body to be a remarkable self-sustaining machine, but nothing more. According to this traditional model, the body and all its trillions of cells is maintained not by invisible interpenetrating energy, but by the brain and nervous system in coordination with our genes. Essentially, this model views the genes coded in our DNA in the nucleus of the cells as the brain of the cell, and the collective brains of each of the fifty trillion cells work together to keep us alive and healthy.

This conventional biochemical model of life with DNA in the lead role has held the forefront for decades. But in reality the model has never been fully understood. Though most geneticists believe that what you need is pre-programmed for every possible outcome from birth through life, they have yet to identify the majority of the programming that would be necessary for this to be true. Many geneticists thought the human genome project would solve the remaining mysteries. The entire human genome was sequenced in 2003, but the results were not at all what the scientific community expected. In a commentary on the surprising results of the human genome project, one of the world's preeminent Nobel prize-winning geneticists, David Baltimore, addressed the issue: "Unless the human genome contains a lot of genes that are opaque to our computers, it is clear that we do not gain our undoubted complexity over worms and plants by using more genes."[35]

Our Genes Are Not Fixed

Failing to find the pre-programming for all of life encoded in our genes forced scientists into a reassessment of how our genes actually work. In response, they established a new and exciting discipline known as epigenetics. Epigenetics is the study of changes in gene function that occur without a change in the actual DNA sequence.

Discoveries indicate that our genes are not fixed—that permanently dormant genes can become active and currently active genes can become inactive. These discoveries in epigenetics cast serious doubt on the dogmatic belief that DNA is the brain of the cell. It looks much more likely that our cells are controlled from another source. We

---

35   See https://www.nature.com/articles/35057267.

also now know that every protein-producing gene is able to produce *many* different proteins. In fact, recent studies have shown we activate and inactivate our genes *routinely*, not just in rare cases.

One specific study looked at a group of more than thirty men and the risk of prostate cancer over three months following an intensive nutrition regimen. They witnessed an up-regulation of forty-eight genes that help the body fight tumors and down-regulation in 453 genes that tend to promote tumors.[36] Another Swedish study of twenty-three slightly overweight men put on a regimen of spinning and aerobics classes twice per week discovered that the men had genetically altered seven thousand genes, or *nearly 30% of all the genes in the entire human genome*, over a six-month period.[37]

We also know that less than 5% of all diseases today stem from single gene disorders, whereas the remaining 95% of all illnesses are related to chronic stress, toxic factors in the environment, and lifestyle choices.[38]

These and other studies show that environmental, mental, and emotional changes can turn on and off thousands of genes previously considered permanently dormant or permanently active. In fact, twins who begin their lives with identical portions of their activated DNA can actually end their lives with significantly different portions of their activated DNA. There is no hard-and-fast coded destiny in our genes. It is actually—and this is crucial—outside influences such as our *behaviors* and possibly even our thoughts and feelings that alter the activation and expression of our genes. We can signal our genes to design our future. You might be wondering what any of this means for you. We will discuss this in the next section.

---

36 See https://www.ornish.com/wp-content/uploads/8369.full_.pdf.

37 See https://www.ncbi.nlm.nih.gov/pmc/articles/PMC3694844.

38 Lipton, Bruce. *The Biology of Belief 10th Anniversary Edition: Unleashing the Power of Consciousness, Matter & Miracles*, Carlsbad, California: Hay House, 2009.

Putting It all Together

Putting all this information together, three eminent quantum physicists, John von Neumann, John Archibald Wheeler, and Eugene Wigner, came up with their shared interpretation known as the von Neumann-Wheeler-Wigner interpretation (vNWWI).[39] This interpretation suggests that thought and consciousness are not just artifacts or biochemical processes of the brain and nervous system but that thought and consciousness are fundamental causative elements of the cosmos. Essentially, it proposes that not only do thought and consciousness exist beyond matter but that *they have the power to create the material world.*

If you've ever studied personal development and achievement, you're no doubt familiar with Napoleon Hill's classic *Think and Grow Rich.* Originally published in 1937, it has sold over 100 million copies worldwide. I picked up that book when I was seventeen, and I knew there was something magical about the ideas in it. The only problem I had was that there was no empirical, scientific data or evidence to back up the steps to riches Hill describes in the book.

Even without this evidence, the book is incredibly powerful and has changed the lives of millions of people. But, for me personally, I've always been digging and hoping to uncover more about why this particular theory Hill put together makes sense. In the book, one of the mysterious primary ideas is that "thoughts held in mind tend to translate themselves into their physical equivalent." There is also a great emphasis on the importance of emotional energy and intensity in combination with the power of imagination. But why? How is this possible? Was he just guessing?

Perhaps Hill was just ahead of his time, because the von Neumann-Wheeler-Wigner interpretation of quantum physics gives us enough information about what's going on with our powerful emo-

---

39   See https://en.wikipedia.org/wiki/Von_Neumann–Wigner_interpretation.

tions and thoughts to understand how we literally do create our own reality moment-to-moment. This phenomenon likely explains what Hill was seeing in action—our thoughts can control our life trajectory.

The First Step to Designing Your Reality

The most basic tangible step to take advantage of the science available to us is to *build a morning routine*. The key purpose of a morning routine is to put you in a proactive and strategic state rather than falling into a default position of reactivity. Your conscious and subconscious mind, as well as your energy levels, are at their optimum immediately following sleep. Thus, it is important that you take advantage of this time. To do so, I would suggest you begin each day by journaling first thing in the morning. This is crucial for training your subconscious mind to bring your goals into reality. It's always best to write down your goals in the affirmative with a date attached to them (e.g., I'll be making $50,000 a month by January 2022).

Pro-Tip: Creating Your Morning Success Ritual

To maximize your performance, here are a few things you can do right when you wake up, in this order:

1. *Drink a half-liter of water to rehydrate yourself.*
2. *Get some form of exercise.*
3. *Eat something healthy that's high in protein and low on the glycemic index to set yourself up for a successful day of nutrition and focus.*

Complete these three things before you plug-in. In other words, you should never check email, browse social media, or watch the news before this morning routine is done. If you plug-in first thing, you will move through the rest of your day in a defensive posture, reacting to other people's issues and problems rather than living your life proactively with intentional focus.

It is extraordinarily valuable to create a routine you are highly likely to do every day. DON'T make the routine complex or cumbersome. Set the bar as low as it needs to be for you to be highly likely to complete it. One thing to note is that if you plan out your ritual, in written form, you're much more likely to do it because you know step-by-step what needs to be done to make it happen. Here is the key secret: make the clear connection between how you are going to use your natural talents, strengths, and inspirational drivers to help create the world you know will be better in the future.

Max Planck, a Nobel Prize-winning physicist, said, "I regard consciousness as fundamental. I regard matter as a derivative of consciousness. We cannot get behind consciousness. Everything that we talk about, everything that we regard as existing, suggests consciousness." It's through our conscious use of thought that we are able to bring our vision into reality. Align your vision for success with your vision for improving the lives of others and the world around you. How can the world be better in a specific and tangible way that you can visualize clearly, and how can you contribute to helping that world come to be? See how the lives of others will be much more abundant in the future because of the value you will provide, and see clearly how other people directly connected to you will become wealthy because of the value you're bringing them as well. Now picture those people in your life as becoming wealthier than even you. This is the key goal. We will create what's called your "Ultimate Scenario for the Future" in the next exercise.

Allow Yourself to Imagine

Nobel Prize-winning physicist Werner Heisenberg said, "The existing scientific concepts cover always only a very limited part of reality, and the other part that has not yet been understood is infinite." It may be hard to accept at first that you are essential to the existence of the physical reality around you. However, the essential role you and I have in the physical reality has been confirmed over and over by science's intelligent observer experiments. A matter wave only behaves like matter when observed by an intelligent observer.

In other words, a particle cannot present into reality as we know it until we observe it. In the world of physics, this phenomenon is known as the *observer effect*. This discovery tells us mind and matter are inextricably related because the subjective mind produces measurable changes in the objective world. At the subatomic level, energy responds to your mind's focused attention and becomes material reality. Your three-dimensional physical body is directed and guided by the non-local, two-dimensional life-force by quantum entanglement, and this whole process is shaped by your moment-to-moment thoughts.

Everything in the material world gives off a specific pattern of energy. Your fluctuating thoughts and emotions change the type of energy you emit moment-to-moment. Your essence is spiritual, you think with your mind, and you live in a physical body powered by your *life-force*. Since thoughts themselves are energy, the electrical impulses generated by the brain can be measured easily by devices such as an EEG, and thoughts are one of the primary methods by which we send out signals to the two-dimensional quantum field.

The scientists at the HeartMath Research Institute[40] have performed lots of research into the physiological part of brain interaction and emotions. They've been able to document a specific link between our heart rhythms and our emotional states. When we experience negative emotions such as living in a state of fear, our heart rhythms become erratic and unpredictable. But when our emotions are positive, such as those we'd experience through love and joy, we produce highly ordered and coherent heart patterns.

---

40   See https://www.heartmath.org/research.

Cellular biologist Glenn Rine, PhD, led a fascinating study at HeartMath. In the experiment, he first studied a group of ten individuals who were well-versed in using techniques that the HeartMath Institute teaches to build heart coherence. They used these techniques to produce strong emotions on the positive side of the spectrum, and then for two minutes they held test tubes containing DNA suspended in deionized water.

When they sampled those specimens, no changes had occurred to the DNA. The second group of trained individuals did effectively the same thing, but instead of creating positive emotions, at the very same time they held an intentional thought to either wind or unwind the strands of DNA. This group produced statistically significant changes in the shape of the DNA samples. In some cases, as much is 25% of the DNA was altered compared to before the experiment. This is another mind-blowing revelation. Only when a subject held both positive emotion and clear intentional thoughts in alignment with the emotion were they able to produce the effect they desired.

It appears that *intense thought paired with positive emotion,* where the heart and mind are united into a coherent state, produces the most effective idealized outcome. If you are able to think about the combination of how you are *thinking* and how you are *feeling* as how you are *being,* you have made a crucial discovery. The discovery is that *your identity drives results.* Put another way, the quickest way to achieve the results you desire is to begin immediately to *be* the type of person in thought and feeling that would produce those desired results. This understanding—that who we are being from moment to moment generates an electromagnetic force that influences every atom in our reality—forces us to think about what energy we are emanating at any given time.

We tend to get this backwards because the classical model has taught us that everything is based on cause-and-effect. We base what's possible for us on both our past results and our current circumstances. We allow our external environment to dictate who we are being. Instead, the evidence suggests that if we change our internal environment, *who we are being*, the external environment will then be molded by us. To be clear, when you DECIDE what your new reality will be like, the clarity and coherence of those thoughts will produce a specific set of powerful emotions. The result will be a change in internal body chemistry and alteration in neurological connections (as the old synapses are pruned away and new ones sprout), as well as new genetic expressions that match your new identity.

A Participatory Universe

Current neuroscience tells us the brain is organized based on all the information we've been exposed to throughout our lives. This includes our experiences, our knowledge, and our environment. The brain stores these connections, or synapses. The networks of neurons that make up your brain reflect all your personal experiences with people, things, and places. In many ways your brain is a record of your past experiences and reflects the life you've lived up to this point. Put another way, if you allow it to, the contents of your brain will direct your future to mimic and be limited by your past results. You don't want this. *You want to strategically design your reality.*

To do this, you must hold in your thoughts an idealized version of the person you want to be, a model that is different from and better than the you that exists today. I'm not saying the current you is inadequate. But you would not be taking the time to read this book unless you wanted to change. Since you made it this far, you must make a clear decision and visualize the person you desire to be and start being that person to design the reality you choose.

If you want to feel more confident, buy clothes that fit well and dress better. Get a haircut you like. Upgrade the equipment in your office. Small tweaks like this can create internal shifts very quickly that will help you design an ideal reality. Unfortunately, most people react to the reality they find themselves in. They haven't made the choice to design their own reality.

The quantum field we have discussed is potential energy with the ability to organize itself into subatomic particles that can then become atoms and molecules, all the way up to everything you see in reality. In terms of your physiology, it organizes molecules into cells, cells into tissues, tissues into organs, and organs into the systems that make up your entire body. The higher frequency energy in the quantum field lowers its frequency until it becomes solid.

As prize-winning physicist John Archibald Wheeler put it, *this is a participatory universe.* And I would add that you must make the decision to actively and strategically participate. Strategically design your reality!

Lose Yourself

We can trace your past challenges and failures to one major downfall: you haven't made a commitment to live by the understanding that each of your individual thoughts have consequences so significant they impact and ultimately create your physical reality. Isn't it interesting that you lose all sense of self and become ego-free whenever you are creating something or doing meaningful work? This is because when you're in a state of creation you're activating your brain's frontal lobe. The frontal lobe has several key functions for designing your reality. Here are three crucial functions that are game-changers:

Self-Awareness: The ability to observe yourself and your thoughts. This allows you to evaluate yourself and make a plan to modify certain behaviors to create more favorable outcomes in the future. Current results are based on past actions.

Rewire Your Brain: The ability to influence the brain to rewire its neural networks. The brain has this ability to rewire and create new circuits at any age as a result of input from either the environment or our conscious intentions (this is called *neuroplasticity*). We create a "new" mind because the frontal lobe has access to all other parts of the brain and connections to it, which allows it to piece together bits of information into networks to facilitate new wiring. By doing this, the mind creates a model or representation you see clearly as your intended future outcome. It uses information from already acquired knowledge. So the greater your knowledge base, the greater your imagination will be at dreaming of more complex models. This is why it's so important to read, learn, and acquire knowledge. The more knowledge you have, the more building blocks are in place for the frontal lobe to interact with to create a new model of reality.

Knowledge Is Ammunition: When you clearly decide on the person you want to be, you can mentally rehearse new ways of being on a regular basis, and the rewiring will begin to take place. If I had to break down the main purpose of reading this book, it would be to recreate a mind that is wired to take you to and keep you in the Top 1%.

Make Thoughts the Ultimate Reality: The ability to make thoughts is more real than anything else. When you're in a mode of creativity and strategic design, the frontal lobe essentially ignores signaling from other areas of the brain and pushes out distractions. The internal world of thought becomes as real or even more real than the outer world. The thoughts are then captured by the brain and integrated as a neurological experience. Remember that the brain can't differentiate between an actual experience and thoughts about an experience. Once you get very good at executing this mental rehearsal in creating reality through your thinking, you can actually produce an emotion with the thinking. This emotionally charged clear vision is what begins to impress the reality you're designing onto your subconscious mind.

The Obstacle of "Learned Helplessness"

In 1965, Dr. Martin Seligman and his colleagues performed research on the process by which an animal or human being associates one process with another. We refer to this as *classical conditioning*. In this particular experiment, the researchers would ring a bell and then deliver a small electrical shock to a dog. After a number of times, the researchers found that the dog would react to a shock even *before* it was delivered. Essentially, as soon as the dog heard the bell ring, he would react as if he'd already been delivered a jolt of electricity.

But then something more unexpected happened. Seligman put each dog involved in the experiment in a crate divided down the middle by a low fence. The dog could see and jump over the fence if necessary. On one side of the low fence the floor was capable of delivering electric shock, but on the other side there was no electricity. Seligman initially placed the dog on the side of the fence that was electrified and administered a small shock. He assumed the dog would simply hop over the low fence to escape the shock. Surprisingly, the dog just lay down. It was as if the animals had learned from the initial part of the experiment that there was nothing they could do to avoid the shocks. In response, they just stopped trying.

Seligman described this behavior as *learned helplessness*.[41] The dogs didn't try to escape a negative situation simply because a past experience had "taught" them they were helpless. To confirm his theory, he did the second portion of the experiment again with a new set of dogs that had not been exposed to the classical conditioning part of the experiment (part 1). These dogs that had not been exposed to the first set of shocks immediately jumped over the low fence to escape the shocks.

Seligman concluded the helpless behavior was indeed a learned practice. Here's why this is important to you. Further research has shown that learned helplessness affects human beings as well. In other words, you and I can learn to be helpless in the face of certain negative situations solely because previous situations have shown us that we have no control. This is not good. This will immediately halt your progress and push you to feel like you don't have autonomy and control over the outcomes of your own life and circumstances. You must overcome the tendency toward this type of poor thinking.

So, armed with the knowledge of learned helplessness, how do you overcome it? First, you need to clearly see the future you're working to create. Then see all the challenges, obstacles, and roadblocks that seem to be in the way of you getting to that vision. After that—this is where most people get tripped up—simply reframe those challenges and obstacles as the necessary causes of your future vision coming into reality. See them as being a necessary part of making you the person who can bring that desired reality into existence.

Giving up is the number one thing that will keep you from bringing your Major Mastery Mission into reality. Giving up is almost always related to a failure, or a perceived failure, of some kind and

---

41   See https://flowpsychology.com/martin-seligmans-learned-helplessness-theory.

your reaction to it. Your reaction to it is almost always some type of negative emotion, so to counteract that negative emotion you must get very good at mastering the positive success emotions of desire, responsibility, gratitude, commitment, and optimism.

Recognize that your mind is a reality-making machine. Essentially your mind is the most sophisticated virtual reality mechanism known to man. Our experience of day-to-day reality relies completely on our mind to construct it in a way that is coherent for us individually. The primal self that lived in Mayhem is no longer there, which frees up an immense amount of energy.

Remember that everything is energy, and energy can't be created or destroyed. That's a law of thermodynamics. Finally, and this is very important, thought is the most efficient form of energy in our universe. Remember all those studies and science we discussed earlier in the chapter? The point of that journey was not academic in nature. Rather, it was to show you that you are armed and equipped with the greatest asset to change the trajectory of your life—the mindful energy to choose your outcomes.

When all that old energy focused on doubt and fear and shame and guilt is freed up, you can then move into higher-frequency emotions, generosity, and selflessness. When we move up this emotional resilience continuum, we feel more connected to our authentic spiritual selves and more in touch with the divine nature given to us by our Creator. When we feel in touch with this divine nature, in connection to our Creator, powerful emotions like faith become much more easily integrated into our person and identity. This is the way life was designed to be lived.

Pro-Tip: Goal Visualization

It is essential to write down and visualize the process of achieving your goals. Research has shown that by visualizing the process, including the obstacles along the way to your goals and how you'll overcome them, your performance will increase and your level of anxiety will decrease. Here's how to do it:

1. *Think about your number one goal and write it down on a piece of paper.*
2. *Give it a timeline for completion (reasonably short).*
3. *Imagine all the potential challenges and obstacles you'll face along the way to achieving the goal.*
4. *Write down the challenges and obstacles.*
5. *Come up with an automatic response you will have to overcome each of those obstacles as they arise.*
6. *Write down those responses to each of the challenges you imagined (the more specific, the better).*

Each of us has the innate tools to create our preferred identity. With the advent of a strong mind powered by infinite energy, we find ourselves in a position like never before. There are no limitations to our abilities to create a remarkable and successful life. Science, as outlined in this chapter, offers us boundaryless potential, and with this new awareness we are now better equipped than ever to architect a life that exceeds all our expectations.

Exercise: Your Strategically Designed Reality

This is where you're going to write the script of the future twenty years from now: how it will be different, how you and those associated with you will be wealthy, and how the world will be a better place because of the value you and those associated with you have created in the world. This exercise should take some time and be very well thought out, maybe several pages long. This is the most powerful exercise you can do for your future.

Because the right hemisphere of the brain is more creative and imaginative than the left, it's so crucial for visualizing and designing your ideal reality. There are a variety of practical ways to capitalize on the power of your mind here. The key is to visualize your ideal future in vivid detail with as much emotional intensity as possible. Leading yourself (and others) and designing your own reality is a never-ending process of keeping your vision, purpose, and inspirational drivers at the forefront of your mind and aligning your actions with them.

Dr. Charles Garfield has done research on peak performance in both the athletics and business realms.[42] One of the key things his research showed was how nearly all world-class athletes and performers in other sectors habitually practice visualization. They see themselves performing in their mind's eye and feel what it will be like to perform at their best in every situation. Research shows that this works very well for things like difficult conversations, daily work challenges, speeches or presentations, and yes, even on the golf course.

For example, maybe there's a particular person at work who is difficult to get along with, but part of staying in alignment with your vision, purpose, and inspirational drivers requires kindness, self-control, grace, and forgiveness. What you can do is create a daily mantra or affirmation that will help you remain in alignment with your ideal vision of reality. You'll write it down in a specific way, then keep it with you until you memorize it and can bring it to the forefront of your mind when the challenging situation arises.

---

42   See https://books.google.com/books/about/Peak_Performers.
html?id=ztKNTGYyqokC.

Chapter 6

BEHAVIOR #5: COMMIT TO MASTERY

The moment one definitely commits oneself,
then providence moves too. All sorts of things occur
to help one that would never otherwise have occurred.
The whole stream of events issues from the decision,
raising in one's favor all manner of unforeseen incidents
and meetings and material assistance, which no man
could have dreamt would have come his way.
~ William Hutchinson Murray ~

Throughout history, men and women have often found themselves trapped by their perceived limitations and a feeling of lack of control over the world around them. But what if I told you we all have an inner "genius" characterized by a latent power that we can access? There is a level of untapped human potential in your soul that is the source of all human achievement. To that end, cultivating this latent potential into genius-level performance requires the behavior I refer to as *Commitment to Mastery*.

The world is complex, without a doubt. So how do Shepherd Leaders deal with this complexity? Well, counterintuitively, they simply ignore it. Instead, with extreme focus they concentrate on their Major Mastery Mission and create a sense of blindness to nearly everything else. I'll be guiding you through the process of creating your personal Major Mastery Mission in this chapter. If you wish to reach Mastery, you must develop a sort of distraction filter. There's simply too much of the world and too little of you for any meaningful progress otherwise.

If you're putting forty minutes into a workout, how can you minimize the downtime and maximize the impact of that workout? If you're giving a presentation, what advanced technique or additional preparation can you do to convey your message with more depth and power? Top 1% performers take the time to ask these questions and then pursue the necessary steps to reach the top. You have to do things a bit differently and with a special type of commitment.

A commitment to Mastery requires patience. It may take five or even ten years before your real results begin to multiply. But trust the process and above all else focus on the Major Mastery Mission that you'll be developing in this chapter. It is your duty to build this muscle. You are a leader, and you must behave that way.

The Navy SEALs have a saying: *You don't rise to the occasion, you sink to the level of your training.* The truth behind this is the more fear or anxiety that enters the equation when you're undertaking something challenging or important, the more norepinephrine that is pumped into your bloodstream, and the smaller the database of neurological pattern recognition accessible to you. In other words, you go into a small-scale fight-or-flight response, and your perceived options and creativity become very limited. You revert to the level of your previous training, whatever that might look like.

If you desire an extraordinary life, you must commit to taking extraordinary measures to create that life. These extraordinary measures don't happen overnight in one miraculous performance, but instead this process of Mastery works much like compound interest in that minute improvements each day, building into each week, building into each month, building into each year create Mastery, expertise, and Top 1% performance.

Attaining Mastery

Can you actually reach Mastery? This is an important question that deserves some reflection. Many people in the world have reached Mastery before you, so we know it is *not impossible*. Perhaps equally important, the people who have reached Mastery were not born with this superhuman talent. Not at all. They were simply people who committed deeply and made a decision to train themselves in a specific way to reach the highest level. It is not about innate talent, it's about what you do with what you have and what you commit to.

Finding contentment and fulfillment in a state of Mediocrity is an exhausting battle. Your focus is to be just a little less average than the person you're competing against, and the constant pain of insecurity and doubt steals the confidence required to do elite-level work in the world.

Because of the overflow of Mediocrity and Mayhem, the opportunities to separate yourself through elite-level work and performance are virtually limitless. And this, as much as anything else, is the value of committing to Mastery.

Creating Separation

There are some relatively simple ways we separate masters from others. When acquiring a new ability, what you're learning may seem impossible. The tendency is to quit because of the frustration that inevitably comes with this discomfort. However, those who reach the level of Mastery don't quit. They push through the frustration and discomfort because they have a deep faith in the process. When it comes to mastering new abilities, time is the necessary ingredient. Most are willing to do new things for a short time, but not long enough to reach Mastery. It is inevitable that you will encounter impatience, insecurity, boredom, and fear. You won't be able to avoid these emotions completely, but what you can do is have deep faith that what you're doing is moving you closer to your Major Mastery Mission. The insecurities will go away and become confidence as you gain more mastery.

Take a minute to think back to what your mind was like in your childhood. Remember how open your mind was to ideas and how everything seemed so exciting and fresh and intense. You had a desire to enjoy yourself and to make everything into a game. When you think back, you can't help but be nostalgic for that intensity and zest you experienced when you interacted with the world. Just think of the magic and beauty of Christmas morning as a kid!

I remember vividly when I was a kid in the 1980s and the World Wrestling Federation (WWF) was my world. At that time, there was a huge event every year called WrestleMania, and I would wait in eager anticipation for WrestleMania to happen. But the kicker was, you had to get it on pay-per-view. You couldn't find it on cable. I would never dare ask my parents at that time to buy something on pay-per-view, so I waited for it to come out on VHS, and we would rent it (back when you could go to the grocery store and rent movies on VHS). My parents would sometimes allow me to rent two or three years' worth of WrestleMania, and I would just binge watch them over and over and over.

At that time, the prime-time players were names like Andre the Giant, Macho Man Randy Savage, The Ultimate Warrior, The Junkyard Dog, and Rowdy Roddy Piper. But without a doubt my favorite was Hulk Hogan. I worshipped the ground Hulk Hogan walked on (I wasn't quite as spiritually mature in those days). I mean, Hulk Hogan's theme song was "I am a Real American." He was the definition of "awesome" to me.

The point I want to make here is that I was so deeply entrenched into the WWF, and Hulk Hogan specifically, that I would physically sweat and throw myself around the room, convinced I somehow had the ability to affect the outcome of those wrestling matches I was watching on the screen. My imagination, and the intensity and openness of mind with which I took in those experiences, is etched into my mind.

I actually got in trouble for trying to "body slam" some of my friends at school, just because it was so clear to me I was destined to be a professional wrestler. That sense of wonder and excitement is unforgettable. Unfortunately, as you and I go through new life experiences, encounter negativity, and receive thousands of different opinions about the world around us, our minds gradually become restricted and resistant to creativity and that sense of wonder. We lose that child-like mentality.

Our primal self kills this creative force and innate imagination through our own attitude. We fall into Mediocrity and become comfortable with our position and the knowledge we already have. We are afraid of failure and afraid of entertaining new ideas and the potential effort involved in changing. Our minds begin to atrophy from the lack of challenge and new experience. Most of all we become limited and surrender control of our reality.

But masters overcome this pull toward Mediocrity by making the decision to attain an incredibly high level of knowledge about their field or specialty while maintaining a willingness to use this knowledge with flexibility and openness in new and different ways. They commit to becoming indispensable and irreplaceable. Just think of transcendent figures like Steve Jobs, Mozart, Einstein, Henry Ford, or Warren Buffett. They all reached the outer edges of human potential not by being born a "prodigy" but by building deep knowledge in their area of interest, remaining open, creative, patient, and—perhaps most of all—by maintaining enough childlike excitement about their work to make all the time and effort necessary pleasurable enough to continue.

Pro-Tip: What Makes You Indispensable and Irreplaceable?

Ask yourself: What is it about you and the way you do your work that makes you indispensable and irreplaceable in the marketplace? Don't be surprised if it takes some time to think this through. You may even need to create this indispensability in some new original way. The point is not to come up with your final answer here but to get your mind moving in the correct way to put you back into creative mode and excited again about reaching the Top 1% in your space.

Flow

Mihaly Csikszentmihalyi,[43] a pioneer in the field of positive psychology, is known as the father of "flow" psychology. He defines flow as a state of being fully absorbed in an activity with laser-like focus, completely "in the zone." This is the feeling that you have a higher level of command of both reality and yourself. Over the course of about fifty years, Csikszentmihalyi conducted hundreds of interviews with geniuses from various domains of expertise. He studied world-class athletes, Nobel Prize-winning scientists, inventors, and award-winning writers.

---

43   See https://en.wikipedia.org/wiki/Mihaly_Csikszentmihalyi.

The commonality he found was that geniuses (or masters) spend their time either pursuing an activity with enormous intensity or engaging in complete restoration and recovery. This specific combination prevents burnout and mental exhaustion, but it also fosters breakthrough ideas and discoveries. He documented this as the following three-step process:

1. *Immersion*: total engagement in their work with deep unrelenting focus.
2. *Incubation*: a period of rest and recovery when they are not at all thinking about the work.
3. *Insight*: the occurrence of "aha" or eureka moments that bring new ideas and expansion into their thinking.

As you're committing to Mastery, the logical question then becomes, how can you use this in your own life to tap into your genius?

Flow is technically defined as an optimal state of consciousness in which you feel your best and perform at your highest level. In the state of flow or "in the zone," your mental and physical levels of performance go through the roof and you also tend to lose track of time. You actually experience something called "time-dilation," which is similar to what happens in the movie *The Matrix*, and you feel like things are in slow-motion. You'll frequently get so engrossed in what you're doing that hours will go by without you even realizing it.

Another thing Csikszentmihalyi discovered was that flow is not an on-and-off type of consciousness but rather a continuum. In other words, you can be in a low micro-state of flow in which a few characteristics are present, or you can be in a state of hyper-flow in which everything is clicking at the highest level. This is similar to what we might describe as a spiritual experience. Csikszentmihalyi also found that flow is not reserved for any specific group or type of people. *Any person, in any field*, can tap into flow as long as an initial set of conditions are in place. This is a crucial point because you now know it is accessible to each of us, and so it becomes your responsibility to figure out how to integrate it into your workflow.

One final thing that Csikszentmihalyi found may be the most important thing to look at when building a life that integrates science, success, and spirituality. He realized that those who found the most *meaning* and *purpose* in their lives, as well as the greatest level of fulfillment, were those who could tap into flow states most consistently. This means that the more flow the high performers had in their lives, the more fulfilled they were.

McKinsey, the business consulting company, found that those who are able to work in a flow state are *five times more productive* than they were when not in a flow state. In essence, those executives they studied who were highly productive and working in a flow state could get as much meaningful work accomplished in one day per week as their counterparts could in five days per week. This is a BIG DEAL.

Where "Genius" Comes From

Through brain studies and functional MRI technology, scientists have been able to figure out what's happening in the brain when you're "in the zone." It's a process called *transient hypofrontality*, or temporary deactivation of the prefrontal cortex. The prefrontal cortex is the front part of the brain responsible for logical decision making, long-term planning, and even morality. Transient hypofrontality allows you to drop deep into the present moment and situation with very little regard (if any) for past- or future-oriented thinking.

This inherently flushes out anxiety and stress-related hormones, taking those factors out of the performance equation. Yet another huge benefit is that the dorsal lateral prefrontal cortex—which houses your sense of self, particularly your critical sense of self where the voice that says "you're not good enough" and "you're not smart enough" and "you can't do this" lives—is effectively shut off when "in the zone" as well. Doubt goes away, fear goes away, and insecurity goes away.

The *beta* wave state is the normal brain wave state when you're just actively awake and thinking throughout the day. The second state is called the *alpha* wave state and is characterized by relaxation physically and mentally. When you're not asleep but just in a pretty relaxed mode, your brain is in an *alpha* wave state. The third brain wave state is *theta*. This is the one where you're fading off to sleep or daydreaming, and it's where REM sleep takes place.

Flow takes you from the *beta* wave state, where you normally are, down to the junction, kind of a meeting point, between *alpha* and *theta* wave states. The magic of this junction point between *alpha* and *theta* that flow produces is how it gives you access to a fourth kind of brain wave known as a *gamma* wave. The *gamma* brain wave state is where neurological binding takes place. This binding is when you get "aha" moments and when multiple different pieces of information from different brain regions click and create breakthrough moments in your thinking. *This is an area or wave state that seems to be very accessible by geniuses on a regular basis.*

The final important discussion point biologically with the flow state is the neurochemical component, specifically related to the release of norepinephrine, dopamine, and serotonin. Norepinephrine and dopamine are very important for intense focus. Serotonin is important for keeping you calm and cool under pressure because it gives you a relaxation feeling. In fact, many antidepressant medications are in the category of SSRIs, or *selective serotonin reuptake inhibitors.*

These drugs inhibit the re-uptake of serotonin so it stays present and up-regulated, more readily providing a feeling of calmness and relaxation. A fourth chemical involved in flow is anandamide, which is important in promoting lateral thinking, or the idea of being able to connect seemingly disconnected ideas into a new coherent idea.

Clearly, this is important in things like invention or creativity of new ideas. The final chemical group is endorphins, which are potent pleasure chemicals and also pain-relieving chemicals that promote social bonding as well.

All five of these are some of the most potent reward chemicals in the brain. They give you pleasure in the sense of feeling rewarded. Here's a key point: *flow states are the only time all five of these chemicals are present at the same time that we know of.* A great example for comparison from a biological standpoint is the feeling of "falling in love." It's that feeling of almost being high from the initial romantic love sensation, which actually only involves norepinephrine and dopamine together. So the flow state is even more powerful because it involves all five chemicals. This provides an inherent motivation for you to get back to the state once you've experienced it before.

Human motivation is always a hurdle in performance, and flow helps you overcome the challenge of motivation by building inherent motivation because of the pleasure chemicals involved. In terms of your ability to learn and convert learning into long-term memory, the general rule neurochemically is that the more neural chemicals involved in a learning process, the more likely the experience is to be moved from short-term memory into long-term memory storage. Consequently, the more you are learning in a state of flow, the more likely you are to learn at a high level and thus gain expertise more quickly.

A cool study that gives credence to this idea involves snipers in target acquisition. The study was done by a group in Carlsbad, California, along with the Department of Defense, in which they trained the snipers on flow and found that when they were trained, they were able to learn target acquisition skills 200% faster than normal.[44] The study has been repeated on other groups such as radar operators and

---

44   See https://www.forbes.com/sites/stevenkotler/2014/01/08/the-research-is-in-a-four-letter-word-that-starts-with-f-is-the-real-secret-to-ultimate-human-performance/#66449073227f.

shown to be accurate. Finally, from the creativity standpoint, studies have shown that flow states increase creativity anywhere between 400% and 700%. These neurochemicals increase pattern recognition and lateral thinking exponentially.

Getting into "the Zone"

This all leads to the question: how do we get into a state of flow? For starters, getting into a flow state requires a deep and intentional state of total focus. As I mentioned earlier in Behavior #4, everything is energy. To achieve and sustain optimal levels of performance, your energy must be channeled in the right ways.

"Passion" is a word that has been used by many of the greats in the field of success and personal development, most notably Tony Robbins, and there are some who find that word to be a bit nauseating and even ridiculous. But it seems to be important in terms of the biological trigger related to reaching "the zone." One of the reasons passion is so crucial is because it helps you push through obstacles and discomfort when you don't necessarily want to. It increases what renowned researcher Angela Duckworth refers to as "grit." In fact, she defines grit as the intersecting point between passion and perseverance.

Passion also promotes deep focus for an obvious reason, which is those things you're deeply connected to and inspired by *draw and keep your attention.* One key component to cultivating passion is discovering what you're really curious and excited about. Both curiosity and excitement combat fear and promote spikes in norepinephrine. Here's a key point to remember: *it's actually difficult, if not impossible, to be profoundly curious and excited about something and fearful and anxious at the same time; they're mutually exclusive emotions.* Fundamentally, this is the act of immersing yourself into the activity.

The next stage is to spend some time diving into those intersection points and learning and giving yourself the ability to interact and cultivate that curiosity in those areas of intersection. You might remember earlier I talked about stage one of Csikszentmihalyi's flow called *incubation*. What you're doing when you study these areas and spend time with them is allowing learning to take place in your conscious mind. When you do this, you're allowing your brain to incubate and make connections for future integration. This time of incubation will build more momentum for you over the long term.

As you dig into your curiosities and connect them up to bolster your level of passion, you will begin to find more flow in your life. But here's the thing with passion: it's primarily *self-centered* and in some ways narcissistic. It's mostly about you. This is not good (see Behavior #3). As a Shepherd Leader aspiring to make a major difference, impact, and contribution to the world, you don't want to stay stuck in a self-centered state of mind.

What you have to do is translate that deep passion, deep curiosity, and those deep connections into a "purpose-driven life" as Rick Warren describes in his book of the same name. Purpose is huge because it brings other people into the fold of the bigger cause you're building, and it's a focusing mechanism (on top of passion). In a sense, you're stacking up mechanisms that push for higher levels of focus which serve to put you predictably "in the zone." You want to do work you love, which is what passion and curiosity cultivate, but on top of that you desperately desire your work to matter to the world and to others. That is what purpose allows.

As we look back at the greatest historical leaders and geniuses, a profound sense of purpose consistently emerges. For Henry Ford it was to become the pioneer in developing an engine- driven automobile. For Albert Einstein it was to understand the unseen forces in the universe and make sense of them. For John Wooden it was to create great men and future leaders by teaching them the game of basketball. And for Martin Luther King Jr. it was a dream of equal rights for all races. It is finally time for YOU to uncover your Major Mastery Mission.

The Power of Autonomy

This pursuit of Mastery offers us the opportunity to live an autonomous life. Autonomy is to be in control of the direction of your life. It's a huge motivator, and people like you and I who have a deep desire to achieve and contribute at a high level are obviously very motivated by the idea of steering our own ship. There are examples of this everywhere.

Patagonia was founded on the principles of Csikszentmihalyi and flow psychology. They brought in this idea of autonomy at a serious level in their company. What they've done is institute a policy called "let my people go surfing," where they will allow their employees to take time away from work to surf whenever they feel it's necessary, which allows them to get exercise, stay motivated, and think more clearly.

On top of that, each employee gets to create their own work schedule around their sleep patterns in terms of when they work best, which is another huge level of autonomy. Consequently, Patagonia's employees are among the most motivated, happy, and fulfilled of any business in the world.

So how does this apply to you? One thing I would suggest you do immediately if you're serious about reaching Mastery is to carve out an hour a day for your Major Mastery Mission. I want you to make that commitment to work deeply on this particular purpose. This will build autonomy because you'll be dictating what you'll do with those four to five hours per week, and it will allow you to begin to develop Mastery, which is your entire goal here.

The book you're reading now, the leadership and performance system this book is based on, as well as the Top 1% podcast I host are each products of the four hours I take per week for autonomy. It has become an intense passion connected to purpose. I want you to do the exact same thing for your own purpose.

Building Your Ladder

You now have this major purpose called your Major Mastery Mission. To pursue this Major Mastery Mission, you'll need to construct a ladder made up of several steps called "Challenging Attainable Goals" (CAGs). These goals should clearly line up with your Major Mastery Mission. They should be both challenging and attainable. So your exercise at this stage is to break your Major Mastery Mission into three to five individual CAGs. For example, if your goal is to start a podcast that changes the world, break that down into three to five challenging but attainable steps you can put into action during your four to five hours a week of autonomy.

The problem with most Alpha 1.0 thinkers is that they are out of alignment with their Top 1% ID and PIL (purpose in life). Most detrimental of all is that they have no clear Major Mastery Mission to guide their life.

The Shepherd Leader overcomes these foundational problems by being philosophy-driven. The Top 1% philosophy directs their behavior and the Major Mastery Mission is their guide. As a Shepherd Leader yourself, I urge you to take the creation of your Major Mastery Mission very seriously. It will make all the difference.

One of the most impactful ways to do this is through pushing your perceived limitations. As William James said, "The human individual thus lives usually far within his limits; he possesses powers of various sorts which he habitually fails to use. He energizes below his maximum, and he behaves below his optimum."

I want to tell you a story about a twenty-eight-year-old endocrinologist by the name of Hans Selye. There was a time when Hans was desperately trying to discover a new hormone. He thought he was making progress on discovering a new sex hormone because every time he injected the rats in his experiments with ovarian extract, they experienced a unique physiological response. It activated their immune systems, and their adrenal cortex got larger. The more he injected, the greater the response was. Unfortunately, he became disappointed as he noticed the exact same response in the rats when injecting benign fluids like saline. So what was really going on here?

Further investigation brought to Selye's attention that any active trauma induced in these rats via injection, shocking, or surgical intervention brought about the same adrenal and immune response. The rats weren't readying themselves for a sexual encounter, they were getting ready for a fight.

We now know this is not unique to rats but is a reaction shared as a stress response in basically every living organism. Over time, however, Selye noticed that organisms adapted to each unique stressor by building up an increased resistance to it. Some stressors could even create positive effects, enhancing the part of the body that was under attack. The lesson here is that stress isn't just harmful but can also serve as a powerful stimulus for growth and adaptation.

Athletes from many sports have used altitude training to prepare for a big match or event, and not just when the event will be played at a high altitude. The air is "thinner" at high altitudes, meaning there are fewer oxygen molecules per volume of air. Every breath they take at a high altitude delivers less of what working muscles require. To compensate for the decrease in available oxygen, one of the body's hormones, erythropoietin (EPO), triggers the production of more red blood cells to aid in oxygen delivery to the muscles. By training at high altitudes, athletes aim to allow their bodies to produce extra red blood cells. Then, they head to a competition at lower elevations to take advantage of their enhanced physiology.

There's a key distinction at play. If the amount of stress is too large or too long in duration, not only will the body fail to adapt positively, it will actually begin to deteriorate or break down. This is what Selye referred to as the "exhaustion stage," and this is what happens to many people today when they're under a state of chronic stress. I referred to this in Behavior #2 when discussing the primal self related the disadvantages of chronic anxiety and depression. In these states the body has elevated inflammation, high levels of cortisol, and begins to rebel and break down.

You see there's a paradox emerging here. Stress is a great enhancer, but only up to a certain point. As international chess prodigy Josh Waitzkin put it: "Growth comes at the point of resistance; we learn by pushing ourselves to the outer reaches of our abilities." Skills and mastery come from just the right amount of struggle.

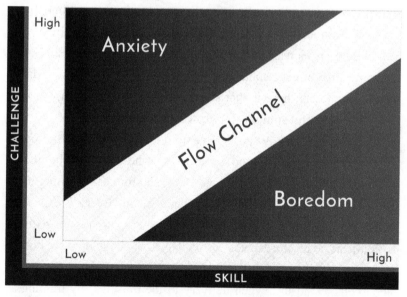

If you desire to continuously improve in whatever you do, you must view stress as something positive and even necessary in your life. It just has to be the ideal amount. The secret to this is to seek out what Brad Stulberg and Steve Magness, the authors of *Peak Performance*, call "just manageable challenges." These are challenges that force you to take on something that makes you feel a bit out of control, but not quite to the point of anxiety. It's a challenge that's at the outermost edges of, or maybe just beyond, your current level of ability. This is the place where your primal self will be whispering "there's no way you can possibly do this." As you now know, this is the voice you ignore because it's trying to pull you back into your security zone. You're not looking for security here, you're looking for Mastery.

An example from my own life comes to mind here. In my residency program I was constantly pushed to the edge of my comfort zone both intellectually and clinically. I was forced into a position to design, execute, and complete a master's thesis, treat patients (many of whom presented with treatment challenges I had never previously encountered), and review immense amounts of literature weekly to present and be ready to discuss when called upon. In fact, all rigorous educational programs such as PhD and medical residencies have figured out the system to drive people to Mastery. It's what they're designed to do.

Every single day of the three-year residency was designed to push me into a position just beyond my current skill level. Of course, at that time I had not studied these concepts, so I didn't understand it this way, but I now understand that to reach Mastery level in the field of endodontics required exactly the type of program I went through. Now having this knowledge, you and I can design these types of scenarios into our lives anytime we choose.

Pro-Tip: Skill Enhancement

Think of a skill or capability you really want to enhance in your life. Now think about what your current level of ability in that arena is. You want to actively seek out challenges that are just slightly beyond your current level of ability, to the point where you feel not quite out of control, but almost. When you reach the point of anxiety, where you're becoming distracted, dial it back just slightly.

The Godfather of Expertise

K. Anders Ericsson, the psychologist considered the world's premier authority on expertise and responsible for a large percentage of studies that have helped determine the specific factors behind top performers, summarized much of his research in his book *Peak: Secrets from the New Science of Expertise.*[45]

Ericsson's initial assumption in the early 1990s was that expertise was primarily related to the right combination of DNA and an accumulation of experience. However, over time he found that the combination of experience and expertise did not necessarily go hand-in-hand. To find out what creates an expert, he put together a team of researchers to study violinists at the Global Music Academy in Berlin, Germany.

The violinists continued doing exactly what they'd always been doing, with the exception that they now had to write down *everything* they did. After seven days, Ericsson compared the records of the highest-level performers to everyone else. He found that all the violinists were practicing about the same amount (roughly fifty hours a week). The key difference was that the top performers spent a much higher percentage of time intensely focused on mastering a specific goal, and they *eliminated all distractions* when doing so. This type of intense and fully engaged practice is what Ericsson has termed "deliberate practice."

One famous "expert" Ericsson examined was Wolfgang Mozart. He wanted to know whether it was innate talent that made him one of the greatest musicians in history. Mozart had perfect pitch from a

---

45   Ericsson, K.A. and Robert Pool. *Peak: Secrets from the New Science of Expertise*, Boston, Massachusetts: Eamon Dolan Books/Houghton Mifflin Harcourt, 2016.

young age. He could hear a note on any instrument and tell you whether it was a B-flat or a C, for example, and which octave the note was in. More impressive, however, is that he could do the same with clocks, sneezes, and other non-musical sounds. At age seven, Mozart dazzled audiences during a tour across Europe. He played the violin, harpsichord, and assorted instruments he'd learned to play from his father's collection. His older sister, Maria Anna, played piano and harpsichord as well. During the European tours, all three of them would perform, but Wolfgang was always the main attraction.

As it turns out, Wolfgang's father, Leopold Mozart, was a music teacher, violinist, and composer and spent many hours teaching his son from four years of age. He was one of the first music teachers to publicly advocate early music instruction. Leopold also instructed Mozart to copy the works of the great artists of the time. By age six, Mozart began composing his own works, and two years later he wrote an entire symphony.

When Ericsson took a closer look at Wolfgang's early instruction and practice, he noticed some peculiarities:

- Wolfgang's early compositions were in Leopold's handwriting. According to Leopold, he was just cleaning and polishing his son's work. No one actually knows what percentage of the work was Mozart's own.
- At age eleven, Mozart wrote some piano concertos, but these were largely based on works by other composers.

The current prevailing hypothesis is that Mozart's early concertos were mainly practice exercises assigned by Leopold to familiarize his son with concerto structures to build a foundation for composition. Evidence also suggests that Leopold played a much larger role in these composition exercises than he led people to believe. And the earliest compositions that experts can truly attribute to Wolfgang were written at age fifteen or sixteen.

According to Ericsson, it's safe to conclude that the bulk of Mozart's talent came from lots of practice and one-on-one training. It's impossible to know this with certainty, but it is captivating to understand that innate talent is minor in the overall picture of *your potential*.

This illustrates an important point. The more you dig into the lives of geniuses, the more a repeated set of circumstances emerges. All these masters had what Napoleon Hill called a "burning desire" to achieve, driven by an inclination toward a field in perfect alignment with their inspirational drivers (their Top 1% ID) and their natural core strengths. They also each served in some sort of apprenticeship or had a high-level mentor who helped push them to the next level (see Behavior #6). Over time, with more deep practice, they experienced their inclination as a deep foundational mission that dominated their thoughts and dreams (this is your Major Mastery Mission). This burning desire is what pushed them through the self-doubt, insecurity, dedication to study and practice, inevitable failures, and ruthless critics. Overall, perhaps the one quality that separates the highest-level masters from everyone else is their ability to be emotionally resilient, confident, and persistent along the path to the Top 1%.

The moment you back off, feeling like you've reached the top of the mountain, the sharpness of your mind will begin to waste away. If Mastery is not continually renewed, you will lose your edge.

Pro-Tip: Eliminating Distractions

Distractions are everywhere, and they will dominate your life if you don't take responsibility for controlling them. One study found that office distractions take up to .1 hours a day, and another study found that employees spend an average of only eleven minutes on a project before being distracted—and it takes twenty-five minutes to return to the original task if it ever happens. Distractions are also exhausting because they rob you of much-needed glucose. External distractions include phones buzzing and beeping, email alerts, and people coming into your office. Internal distractions include something called ambient neural activity.

This is your nervous system constantly reconnecting and reorganizing the trillions of neural connections in your brain at any given moment, and it's why weird thoughts pop into your head at inopportune times. A study done in 1983 by Benjamin Libet found that once you become aware of a desire to do a voluntary activity or movement, your brain made this decision 0.3 seconds (and millions of connections) prior. After that point, there are 0.2 seconds in which you are aware of the desire but have yet to take action. This is the 0.2 second window in which you have the responsibility to intervene.[46] *Here are some suggestions to leverage this knowledge:*

1. *When you need to focus, remove all external distractions, no questions asked.*

2. *Remove the likelihood of internal distractions by clearing your mind before doing meaningful work (see Quadrant Breathing in Behavior #2).*

3. *Make a conscious habit of noticing, labeling, and vetoing distracting thoughts immediately before they take on momentum.*

Ritualize Your Work

To better solidify this journey, it's important that you begin to ritualize your work and be very specific about your environment when working. Writer Stephen King says, "Don't wait for the muse. Your job is to make sure the muse knows where you are going to be every day from nine until noon or seven until three. If he knows I assure you he'll start showing up. Your schedule exists in order to habituate yourself."

King is meticulous about his environment and the consistency of his routine, and as a result he is one of the most prolific writers of all

---

46   See https://en.wikipedia.org/wiki/Benjamin_Libet.

time. Similarly, the great psychologist B.F. Skinner started and ended his writing sessions with the buzz of a timer. He used the power of routine to help him think through and develop the psychological theories underpinning what he called *behaviorism*.

The idea of this rigorous routine building is to make it more automatic for you. Just as a great free-throw shooter or tennis star has a specific routine just prior to shooting a free-throw or delivering a serve, you should execute the same routine every time prior to doing your meaningful work.

Pro-Tip: Work Session Hacks

Here are a few key things to build into any work session:

1. *Be consistent in executing the same routine every time prior to your work session (for example, you may want to do a prayer or meditation, or even a deep breathing exercise for two or three minutes prior to your work).*
2. *Strive to link certain activities to the same time of day, physical environment, and location for additional consistency and familiarity.*
3. *Drink the same beverage or burn the same candle or do something similar that will give you familiar tastes, sights, feels, and smells each time you do your work (I always drink the same type of coffee, for example, and do my work on the same device if at all possible).*

Daniel Coyle shared his discoveries about how to become an expert in his books *The Talent Code* and *The Little Book of Talent*. He developed much of the theory about *deep practice* by visiting "talent hotbeds" that produced world-class performers in a diverse range of fields. But it's worth noting that many of the principles of deep practice and deliberate practice overlap. You could even say the two terms are interchangeable. The main difference is that

Ericsson and Coyle each learned, or invented, a different but similar set of insights and tips for making practice successful. This makes sense because both have different experiments and experiences to draw from.

Coyle's adventures at the talent hotbeds allowed him to interact with many world-class performers and their teachers. He visited a Russian tennis club, with only one court, that has produced more top-twenty female players than the US. He visited elite music schools and received a lot of guidance on how to improve skills.

Ericsson designed many of the psychological studies that experts of expertise and top trainers use to design training programs in their fields. He also interviewed people in a variety of fields to help them create professional development programs, workshops, and university curricula that advanced those fields.

The main thing that makes deep practice and deliberate practice interchangeable is that each of the two authors reads, and learns from, the other's work. The two systems are widely considered one theory. I believe the combination of the two put into consistent practice will be your most efficient way of breaking through "the line of limitation" and into Mastery.

Let's look at some of the principles about deep practice that Coyle solidified during his travels.

Ignition. Ignition is the moment you become inspired to learn a skill and identify with it. You may be dazzled by a musical performance that inspires you to start mandolin lessons. Ignition moments increase motivation, bring a deep sense of joy, and inspire action. Albert Einstein's father bought him a compass, and Albert became fascinated by its magic. Biographer Walter Isaacson quoted him in *Einstein: His Life and Universe*: "I can still remember—or at least I believe I can remember—that this experience made a deep and lasting impression on me. Something deeply hidden had to be behind things."

Engraving and Stealing. Engraving is when you watch and/or listen, intensely and purposefully, to someone performing a particular skill over and over again. This might be a video of a Tiger Woods golf swing or an incredible presenter whose stage presence you'd like to emulate. A lot of chess players use engraving when they watch videos of classic games between world-class players, and then re-enact the games move by move. Coyle brings up examples of speakers listening to famous inspiring speeches and then emulating them, right down to the subtlest inflections in voice tone. After listening to the desired speech enough times, it's easy to catch yourself whenever you stray from the standard of the original speech.

Engraving is intense by nature. You want to imagine yourself doing what your model speaker is doing. You want to feel every little movement and rhythm. You want your observations to become subtler. Watch for a singer's minute lip movements and shapes during certain notes. Measure the pause lengths between a stand-up comedian's jokes. What are the effects of particular pause lengths? How are your subtle movements or pauses different, and how can you improve?

Think of engraving as a subcategory of the Case Method, which is a method built on learning by doing, aiming to be a process of real-world preparation through modeling hypothetical situations. Stealing means copying other people in your field. Pablo Picasso copied many classical works before developing the unique style of surrealism that he became famous for. The Beatles stole some of their vocal sounds from Little Richard. A lot of new garage bands who write original songs initially steal elements from their favorite songs and bands. All great artists have used "stealing" as a practice before eventually mastering their own styles, and, in fact, Picasso considered it a sign of a great artist.

Long-Term Practice in Fewer Sessions. Coyle also emphasizes the benefit of short sessions. Just as in meditation, it's much better to practice for one hour, seven days per week, than for seven hours, one day per week, because this builds a momentum. This is true of many other disciplines too. Shorter but more frequent sessions give your brain time to create the necessary connections. Ericsson found that the greatest performers generally work in chunks of sixty to ninety minutes separated by short breaks. A recent international study done by a social media company called the Draugiem Group found that all store workers had a particular routine: they spent fifty-two minutes deeply focused in their work before taking a seventeen-minute break.[47] Other companies have analyzed the work of their highest-performing employees, and independent of the job or industry, chunks of hard work followed by quick breaks yield the best performance.

Embrace the Struggle and Reframe It

The feeling of struggle and the thought *I've almost got it* are signs of your brain creating new connections between neurons. UCLA's Robert Bjork coined the term "desirable difficulty," which means going beyond your comfort zone with the goal of bringing that activity into your new comfort zone. Stretching yourself to achieve builds and strengthens the right connections in your brain. Instead of framing it as "I hope I don't screw it up this time," reframe it as "I'm going to nail it this time." To help with positive framing, Coyle also recommends visualizing your brain forming new connections between neurons and new circuits.

In 1908, scientists Robert Yerkes and John Dodson discovered a fact about human performance they called the "Inverted-U." They found that performance was poor at lower levels of stress, hit a sweet spot at reasonable stress levels, and tapered off when stress got too high. As Czikszentmihalyi pointed out in his work, it actually takes

---

47 See https://www.cioinsight.com/blogs/to-be-more-productive-work-fewer-hours.html.

a certain amount of stress to help focus your attention and enhance your performance.

Amy Orenstein, a neurobiologist from Yale, discovered that whether or not a synapse in the prefrontal cortex fires correctly depends mainly on having just the right levels of dopamine and nor-epinephrine. When these chemicals are too low you'll feel bored, and if they're too high you'll experience excess anxiety and stress. This is important to know because there are techniques you can use to modify the levels of these chemicals in your body. To become more alert and on your game, a quick strategy is to bring urgency to your task.

Visualizing an activity brings about a similar physiologic response to actually performing the activity. If you're not quite alert enough, you can bump up your level of norepinephrine by imagining something going wrong in the future. Introduce just a little fear into the equation and you'll wake right up. For example, you can imagine being unprepared for an important meeting with a client or missing an important phone call that cost you a life-changing opportunity. Heavyweight champion Evander Holyfield used to imagine how entering the ring unprepared could get him killed, and that served as his motivation to train like a madman.

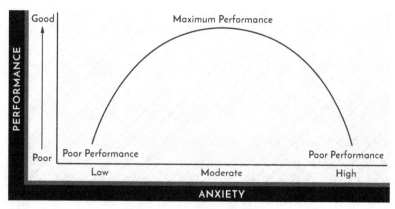

In my own life, the larger problem has been *too much* arousal, which produces heightened anxiety and uncomfortable levels of stress. Over-arousal means there's too much electrical activity happening in the prefrontal cortex. One option here that works well is journaling. Journaling helps reduce the speed of information flowing into your mind and takes those pieces of information out of your head and into the world on paper. Another strategy that works well for me is activating the motor cortex by doing something physical. This could be taking a walk or doing a hard workout, but it makes the oxygen and glucose flow away from your prefrontal cortex, thereby reducing your anxiety. It's a great technique.

Optimizing Your Brain Circuitry

As mentioned, most people, even neuroscientists, once believed that learning was limited to childhood and that your brain is essentially "fixed" by the time you reach early adulthood. However, neuroscience has now proven that lifelong learning is entirely possible and essential to the pursuit of new knowledge and skills throughout life. This concept is known as neuroplasticity.

Your neurons have the potential to physically change the structure of your brain by rewiring themselves throughout your life. This increases the size of localized areas in the brain, as well as the speed with which those regions communicate with one another. Thus, we can always be evolving, developing, and learning. There is no glass ceiling, only opportunity.

In a fascinating study from 2006, a group of researchers scanned the brains of a group of London cab drivers using MRI technology. They followed this up with the same protocol for a group of the city's bus drivers. They then repeated the scans on both groups two years later. Amazingly, they found that a region of the brain associated with spatial learning called the posterior hippocampus had increased in size in the group of cab drivers, while the same region in the bus drivers showed no change.[48]

---

48 See https://www.ncbi.nlm.nih.gov/pubmed/17024677.

What was the cause of the brain changes in the cab drivers? Well, unlike the bus drivers, who used the same route each day over and over, the taxi drivers were forced to navigate new areas of London's challenging geography, day in and day out. By forcing their brains to find new ways around the city, their brains responded by generating more and more neurons. In short, their brains actually expanded to allow for the new information. We can continue to gain new skills and abilities into adulthood, and the regions of our brain responsible for "knowing" things—commonly known as gray matter—will increase in size to help make this process happen. White matter provides all the connections in the brain. As the amount of white matter in the brain expands, the speed at which neurons can communicate with one another increases.

When people learn new skills, whether they be playing chess or leading teams, they will show an increase in white matter as they become more advanced. Essentially, the fluidity with which communication happens between different regions of the brain improves more and more as the skill is perfected.

Neuroplasticity, or the brain's ability to form and reorganize synaptic connections, is key here. Dr. Michael Merzenich explains how learning actually changes the structure of your brain, and these changes further enhance our ability to learn. It seems there is an actual skill we could term "learning how to learn," and Dr. Merzenich makes a couple of interesting observations about better learning.

First, you should never multitask. There are many reasons for this, but among them is the fact that paying close attention is critical to long-term change in brain circuitry. Long-lasting changes in neuroplasticity rely on dopamine, norepinephrine, and acetylcholine. Norepinephrine serves to keep you alert while the rewards that learning brings lead to the release of dopamine and acetylcholine—which in turn ensure the longevity of the neuronal changes. It is also better to dedicate two or three hours of intense focus to a skill than to spend eight hours of more diffuse concentration upon it. You want to get into what Cal Newport calls a "deep work" state, where you are as immediately present to what you're doing as possible.

As your brain hardwires skills and makes certain actions automatic, you will gradually free up mental space to observe yourself as you practice and identify areas that need improvement. Over time, as you develop more and more mastery, you will transform yourself in the process. You will develop more resilience, become more emotionally stable and mature, and your sense of what is pleasurable will even change. The confidence in your abilities, the progress you're making in your skills, and overcoming obstacles and challenges will be the ultimate source of pleasure, as opposed to the immediate dopamine spikes offered by superficial distractions. *There is no more powerful drug on the planet than meaningful achievement.*

Like any physiologic reality, there are downsides to neuroplasticity. Bad habits can change the brain just as readily as good habits. The classic example of this is in golf. If you're not yet a golfer but are thinking of taking up the sport, trust me when I say you should invest in lessons now rather than wait until after you've had the chance to play and develop bad habits. Since bad habits literally rewire your brain circuitry, they are incredibly difficult to unlearn. Once you've developed an inopportune hip movement or improper grip on the club and practiced it for a while, these habits will be stored in your basal ganglia. These facts help explain a lot about my unfortunate golf game (had I known how this process works, I NEVER would have touched a golf club without lessons from a professional from day one—lesson learned).

Applying the Principles of Deliberate Practice
When you create a "chunk," like a golf putt for example, and practice the perfect motion, you're not only reinforcing a circuit but also refin-

ing it. As you practice, that circuit becomes more precise, myelin coats the "wires" in that circuit, and you grow new connections between neurons as well, forming new paths, and these get reinforced with myelin. Thus, this act of deliberate practice can create amazing paths to perfection.

When you reach beyond your comfort zone with a new guitar fingering drill, you're forming a brand-new circuit. As you keep practicing, it becomes more and more refined. The axons get coated with increasing amounts of myelin. Soon it feels natural and you don't have to think or struggle as much to get the right note combinations and make them sound good. Particular parts of your brain thicken when you do this. New neural connections and circuits are characterized by thickened grey matter. Myelin sheaths are associated with what is called white matter.

When you're a child, myelination is rampant. During a certain age range, you can learn a language easily, but it also means if you haven't learned one before the age of twelve, you may have a much harder time. Normally, you start learning a language as an infant and begin talking at age two or three. Kids from immigrant families who have learned the language from their country of origin have a much easier time learning the new country's language than their parents. Myelin is responsible for this.

Children are like sponges for information and are typically very curious. During this phase, they produce a lot of myelin. But as you age, the process slows down. Some skills could be a little harder to learn as time passes. Others will be a lot harder, and it's best to learn them during what are called "critical development times."

This is just your brain's default, however. You can produce myelin throughout your entire life and master many skills. You can also grow new synapses at any time. Many have proven this through deliberate practice.

Pro-Tip: Deliberate Practice Hacks

Here's a practice to start incorporating every time you sit down to do meaningful work, which should be all of your work:

1. *Set a list of concrete objectives for the session.*
2. *Single-task: numerous studies confirm that the quality and quantity of your work suffers when you multitask.*
3. *Create an environment of deep focus and concentration.*
4. *Work in chunks of sixty to ninety minutes separated by short ten- to twenty-minute breaks.*
5. *Physically remove your smartphone from the area where you're doing your focused work.*

Your Brain on Exercise

In the city of Naperville, Illinois, a group of physical education teachers[49] conducted an educational experiment on nineteen thousand students in Naperville School District 203. The experiment took place in gym class, but this was no ordinary gym class. This class is called Zero Hour PE, and its name refers to its scheduled time prior to first period. The objective of the Zero Hour classes was to determine whether working out prior to school hours gave the participants a leg up in academic work and reading ability.

It is becoming clearer that exercise provides an unparalleled stimulus for the brain and primes it to be ready to soak up information. Aerobic activity specifically has a dramatic effect on adaptation and is an indispensable tool for reaching one's full potential.

At the end of the semester this group of Zero Hour PE experimental students showed a 17% improvement in reading and comprehension compared with 10.7% improvement among the other literacy students who slept in and took regular gym class. In Naperville 203,

---

49 See https://www.ou.org/life/health/one-small-change-turned-these-19000-students-into-fittest-smartest-us-alan-freishtat.

the physical education department teaches fitness rather than sports, and the underlying idea is that they're really teaching a lifestyle for a longer and happier life.

An additional piece of evidence that this program is working well for Naperville comes from a test called Trends in International Mathematics and Science Study (TIMSS), designed to compare students' knowledge levels from different countries in math and science. TIMSS has been administered every four years since 1995. The 1999 test looked at 230,000 students from thirty-eight countries, including the United States. Naperville 203 signed up to be part of the exam, and 97% of its eighth-grade students took the exam (not just the most academically advanced). So how did they do? On the science section, Naperville students finished first (as in number one) in the world, just ahead of Singapore. On the math section, Naperville scored sixth behind Singapore, Korea, Taiwan, Hong Kong, and Japan. It seems Zero Hour PE is contributing in a powerful way. So let's figure out why.

It turns out that in addition to priming our state of mind, exercise influences learning directly, at the microscopic level, improving the brain's ability to navigate new topics and understand new information. Remember, we now know that the brain is malleable and not static. Just as muscles are grown by lifting weights, the more we use our brains the stronger and more flexible they become. Every action we take and every thought we think is controlled on some level by how our brain cells, or neurons, connect to each other.

The brain is made up of 100 billion neurons that communicate using chemicals of different types to control every thought and action we perform. Over 80% of the signaling in the brain is done by two neurotransmitters that work to balance one another: glutamate prompts activity to start a new signaling cascade, and gamma-aminobutyric acid (GABA) closes activity down. Interestingly, the more often a connection is activated between two neurons, the stronger the attraction becomes, which is what neuroscientists refer to as binding. This process is prompted by glutamate, and consequently glutamate is crucial in the learning process.

Although glutamate is a powerhouse neurotransmitter, neuroscientists tend to focus more on a separate group of neurotransmitters that have the main function of regulating the signaling process. These other three transmitters are dopamine, norepinephrine, and serotonin. These neurotransmitters can signal directly just like glutamate, or they can adjust the flow of signaling and fine-tune the neurochemistry involved, which is their primary role.

Growing Through Learning

In addition to the neurotransmitters, there is a family of proteins called "factors" that serve the role of building and maintaining the infrastructure of cellular connections in the brain. By far the most well-known of these is called brain-derived neurotrophic factor (BDNF). The process of learning necessitates increasing the strength of neuronal connections through something called long-term potentiation (LTP). When the brain senses it is responsible for taking in new information, it causes the activity of neurons to increase, which in turn strengthens the attraction between the neurons.

Now here's the really interesting part: If the activity continues, genes inside the nucleus of the cell are turned on so they will make more building block materials for the synapses, and the reinforcement of the infrastructure that BDNF is responsible for allows the new information to be captured as a memory.

For the purposes of learning, increasing expertise, and maximizing your potential, the most notable discovery—which earned Columbia University neuroscientist Eric Kandel[50] a share of the Nobel Prize

---

50   See https://www.nobelprize.org/prizes/medicine/2000/kandel/facts.

in 2000—is that repeated activation, or practice, causes the synapses themselves to get larger and make stronger connections. This is a process referred to as *synaptic plasticity*, and BDNF is a main workhorse in the process.

Carl Cotman, director of The Institute for Brain Aging and Dementia at the University of California, Irvine, designed the study responsible for helping us understand that exercise elevates BDNF throughout the brain. Cotman also says "one of the prominent features of exercise which is sometimes not appreciated in studies, is an improvement in the rate of learning, and I think that's a really cool take-home message because it suggests that if you're in good shape, you may be able to learn and function more efficiently."[51]

In 2007 a group of German researchers found that people learn new vocabulary words 20% faster after exercise than they were able to before exercise, and that the speed of learning correlated with the levels of BDNF. On top of that, people with a gene variation that does not allow them to have BDNF are more likely to have learning deficiencies.[52]

The above findings, among others, are what prompted Harvard psychiatrist and author Dr. John Ratey to refer to BDNF as "Miracle-Gro for the brain."[53]

Repeated Rehearsal

The acts of mental rehearsal plus strategic embodiment can often create a new identity for you. But it's not enough to have your mind and body working together just one single time. The question really

---

51 Cotman, C.W., Berchtold N.C. "Exercise: a behavioral intervention to enhance brain health and plasticity," *Trends in Neurosciences*, 25(6) 2002, pp. 295-301.

52 Lang UE, Hellweg R, Seifert F, Schubert F, Gallinat J. "Correlation between serum brain-derived neurotrophic factor level and an in vivo marker of cortical integrity," *Biological Psychiatry*, 62(5), 2007, pp. 530-5.

53 Ratey, John J., Hagerman, Eric. *Spark: The Revolutionary New Science of Exercise and the Brain*. New York: Little, Brown and Company, 2008.

is this: Can you repeatedly embody and mentally rehearse the quality and characteristic that is consistent with the person you want to become regardless of the conditions in your environment at any given time? That is how we create mastery over things in our lives—repetition, or doing the same thing again and again to reach perfection in that skill.

A principle in neuroscience called Hebb's Law explains that nerve cells that fire together (i.e., at the same time) can often wire together or become connected to one another. This law demonstrates that if you repeatedly activate the same nerve cells again and again, each time they turn on will make it easier for them to be activated together the next time. It is a familiarity of sorts. The neurons in this network effectively create a long-term interconnectedness. The more these groups of neurons fire through thought, behavior, or feelings, the more the sensation involved will become automatic and unconscious.

So if you keep thinking the same thoughts, doing the same things, and feeling the same intense emotions you will begin to wire those things into your brain in a permanent and possibly subconscious pattern. For better or worse, you will become attached to the repeated conditions in your life neurochemically. This is the reason people get stuck and stagnant in their lives. The process is predictable. They allow themselves to give up control of their own reality by allowing external conditions to make them a victim rather than a creator (see Behavior #1).

Those who have achieved Mastery such as Thomas Edison, Leonardo da Vinci, John Wooden, Abraham Lincoln, Henry Ford, Steve Jobs, or Jeff Bezos have mastered the idea of a future reality that already existed somewhere and was ready to be created. They all had a dream, vision, and mission that was *much* larger than them as individuals. They believed in a powerful future destiny that was very real in their own minds and behaved daily as if it were already reality. This posture shifted them into being a person who crafted reality rather than a person being dictated to by external circumstances.

Another clear distinction of these individuals was the clarity in their minds about exactly what they wanted their future to look like. Most, in fact, would call these people unrealistic or even outrageous in terms of their future vision. In many ways that was true because the events they embraced in their thoughts, actions, and deepest emotions had not yet occurred in reality.

A 1995 study published in the *Journal of Neurophysiology* followed a set of research subjects that were instructed to mentally practice one-handed piano exercises for two hours a day for five days without ever actually touching any piano keys. This group showed nearly the same brain changes as people who performed the same finger movement on the piano keyboard for the same length of time. Functional brain imaging showed that all the research participants, regardless of which group they were in, activated and enlarged chunks of neurons in the same specific area of the brain.

This study definitively shows that when you are hyper-focused and single-minded, *the brain cannot tell the difference between the internal world of your mind and what you're actually experiencing in the external environment*. Your thoughts can become your experience. Through this type of mental rehearsal, in which you repeatedly think about something with intensity to the exclusion of everything else, you change your brain's wiring to reflect your thinking.

When You'll Know

You'll know you've reached Mastery level when your chosen thoughts and feelings have become so emotionally and chemically ingrained in you that nothing in the external world can overpower your internal control of who you are being in any given situation. Remember that the proper order to produce the qualities of the Shepherd Leader include the acts of *be, do, have.* So the person you and I are being in any given moment is the most crucial aspect because the being will create the doing, and the influence, income, and achievements will be the natural byproducts. So how do we predictably create this sense of being from moment to moment? The Mastery Process is the model I've created for this.

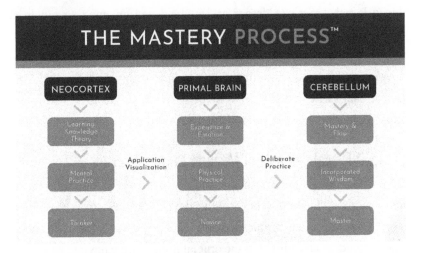

You'll notice that this is an all-encompassing process involving multiple parts of the brain organized in a strategic way to create an incorporated wisdom that is deeply ingrained within us to create mastery. We move from mental rehearsal or physical practice and experience through a period of what Daniel Coyle and Anders Ericsson call *deliberate practice* into what I'm calling *incorporated wisdom.* This leads to ultimate mastery of yourself.

As we discussed earlier, we can't just think our way into a life change. It's the combination of our thinking along with our emotionally deep-seated feelings that will allow us to design the reality we're striving toward.

You have brilliance in you, and the contribution you're meant to make is unique and invaluable. For far too long we have all been programmed into the idea that fitting in and following the 99% is the best way forward. But that path leads only to desperation and discontent. If mediocrity was what you were looking for, you would never have picked up this book.

The original American dream was work hard, follow instructions, be there on time, don't complain—and the rewards will come. But that original American dream has evolved and changed so much it really no longer exists. The new dream, which isn't limited to America, is to create something meaningful, be generous, contribute, and develop deep, strong, and meaningful relationships. In a nutshell, the new dream is to live life on your own terms. To do this, you must adopt Behavior #5: Commit to Mastery.

EXERCISE: Major Mastery Mission Completion

Connecting your deep passions and curiosities and building them into a purpose is simple, but it will take some thinking. Write down five to ten important problems you'd love to solve in your lifetime. These could be anything, but the crucial thing is they have to be really important to you personally. It could be solving problems in the foster care system or solving challenges for small business owners or dealing with challenges students have paying down debt. Anything you're deeply connected to that you would love to help solve can go on this list. Now I'm going to ask you to pick ONE problem or combination of problems on this list to solve. This is now your Major Mastery Mission.

Ultimately, the goal here is to learn how to build this purpose connected to both passion and curiosity into something that can earn you a living. That's the Holy Grail because that's where your real flow will be able to be accessed over and over, day in and day out.

Chapter 7

BEHAVIOR #6:
RELENTLESSLY INVEST IN "THE BIG 3"

There is no enjoying the possession of anything valuable
unless one has someone to share it with.
~ Seneca ~

D id you know that the most iconic movie line in history—"May
the force be with you"—was originally written as "may the
force of *others* be with you." As happiness researcher Shawn
Achor points out, this little line highlights the problem undergirding
our broken search for potential as a society, as well as the secret to
exponentially increasing our success, well-being, and happiness. As

Achor puts it, "We spend the first 20 years of our life being judged and praised for our individual attributes and what we can achieve alone, when, for the rest of our life, our success is almost entirely interconnected with that of others."[54] It turns out almost every attribute of your potential, from intelligence to creativity to leadership, is interconnected with others.

One of the most fascinating studies to support this comes from the *Journal of Experimental Social Psychology*, where researchers found that if you are looking at a hill and judging how steep it is, having the presence of social support around you literally transforms your perception.[55] In fact, if you look at a hill standing next to someone you consider a friend, the hill looks 10% to 20% less steep than if you're facing the hill alone. The results of the study hold even if the friend is three feet away, facing the opposite direction, and silent. Essentially, the study shows that perception of your objective physical world is transformed merely by including other people in your pursuit of achievement. You can reach the Top 1%, but you can't do it alone. As one of my heroes, the late coach John Wooden, once wrote, "The main ingredient of stardom is the rest of the team."

You and I know intuitively that there is something incredibly sad and misguided about a reclusive existence. Life without relationships is fragile, empty, and meaningless. In fact, the process of creating a good relationship is one of the most powerful personal growth tools available to you. It requires you to be generous, vulnerable, courageous, selfless, and faithful. It requires all of you to be successful at the highest level. Perhaps that is why Freud called love "the great educator." Friendships and intimate relationships are always teaching, and if you are astute, you'll always be learning something new.

---

54   See https://www.success.com/how-to-envision-and-reach-your-big-potential.

55   Schnall, S., Harber, K.D., Stefanucci, J.K., & Proffitt, D.R. (2008). Social support and the perception of geographical slant. *Journal of Experimental Social Psychology, 44 (5)*, 2008, pp. 1246-1255.

On your own, you are only a small percentage of your greatest potential. *You feel that deep inside.* You can't be a Shepherd Leader without a team and support system to share the journey. You need them as much as they need you (perhaps more). That is why Behavior #6 is the act of investing in the "Big 3"—your tribe, value-producing assets, and your own education. In each of these investments we find a remarkable return, one that will offer us an exciting opportunity to achieve our dreams and reach out goals.

Your Tribe

Many studies on human interaction and connection demonstrate just how important your tribe is to your overall success. The great Jim Rohn famously said, "You are an average of the five people you spend the most time with." Studies show it is far more common for one delinquent underachiever to bring an entire team down a level in performance than it is for one high-achieving superstar to improve the performance of a group of degenerate peers. Easing up and falling down is a lot easier than buckling down and rising up.[56]

If you choose the right people to surround yourself with, they'll make you better by encouraging you when you're performing at a high level, and they'll call you out with integrity when you're screwing up. If you choose your close relationships poorly, they will sabotage your progress, encourage you to remain in mediocrity (or worse), and they'll be envious of you should you succeed. You must surround yourself with individuals who provide an ideal toward which you feel compelled to strive. Remember, it's your mission to live in such a way that when others see how you conduct yourself, they feel a stirring in their souls to do more, to be more, and to shoulder a larger burden.

56 Barrick, M.R., Stewart, G.L., Neubert, M.J., and Mount, M.K. "Relating member ability and personality to work-team processes and team effectiveness," *Journal of Applied Psychology,* 83, 1998, pp. 377-391.

As Stanford University professor and stress expert Dr. Kelly McGonigal said, "The basic biology of feeling connected to others has profound effects on stress physiology." The positive effects of connecting socially include shifting the nervous system into recovery mode, releasing hormones such as oxytocin and vasopressin, which have anti-inflammatory and anti-oxidant properties, and even increasing heart rate variability. The fact is, even though we may not always want to be social, the benefits of surrounding ourselves with meaningful relationships and enjoying them are huge, particularly following demanding situations.

The United States Air Force Academy conducted an interesting study back in 2010. The goal of this study was to understand why some cadets increase their fitness during their time at the academy while others don't. At the academy, each individual is randomly assigned to a squadron of about thirty cadets prior to starting their freshman year. And once in their squadrons, cadets eat, study, work out, and sleep together. All the squadrons have the same training and recovery regimens, but some squadrons showed major increases in fitness over the four years of training while others did not. What the study figured out was that the major factor in whether the cadets improved was the motivation of the least fit person in each group. If the least fit person had a high motivation to get better, then enthusiasm spread from that person to others in the group, and everyone improved. If the least fit person was lazy or had a negative attitude, everyone else in the group was pulled down.

Another fascinating group of studies show that if one of the people in your group of friends becomes obese, you are fifty-seven times more likely to become obese yourself. If a friend of one of your friends becomes obese, your odds of gaining weight will increase by twenty percent. This is called a negative secondary connection. And regarding smoking, if you have a friend who quits smoking cigarettes, the chances that you'll smoke decrease by thirty-six percent. But even if a friend of one of your friends starts smoking, it raises your chances of becoming a smoker by eleven percent. This is alarming stuff! It's clear the makeup of your close relationships has serious implications on your behavior, and subsequently your performance in life. As we've seen, what you do, how you do it, and even when you do it is crucial, but *who* you choose to align yourself with throughout the process is equally important. You must recognize the enormous power of your tribe.

Dan Sullivan, founder of Strategic Coach®, advises to surround yourself with people who remind you more of your future than your past. This next part is going to be difficult to hear. But you must decide to remove yourself from any relationships that are not in line with your life vision. I understand how difficult this seems and how harsh it sounds, but the impact your relationships have on your behavior cannot be understated. You don't have to ostracize certain people or run them off, but you'll have to build strategic boundaries with individuals who are keeping you from making positive progress. Again, I'll reference Dan Sullivan here, and his advice is that the best thing you can do for these people is to be an example for them. Envision yourself as a role model to the people in your life, because you can't be a role model by living below your potential. In other words, don't stoop to the level of those holding you back, but reach your hand down and pull them up.

Your tribe is a matter of survival. In the 1960s, Abraham Maslow developed his famous "hierarchy of needs." Social connection sits right in the middle of the hierarchy. But the good Dr. Maslow might have been wrong on this one. Many studies are now showing that the brain responds to social needs with the same networks it uses for basic survival. Being hungry activates the same neurological threat and pain response as the feeling of being alienated by a social group. A feeling of relatedness is a reward for the brain, whereas the absence of relatedness generates a threat response. This is why it feels so good to be part of a cohesive and high-performing team. And why you must build and strengthen the connections within your tribe to support Mastery within the group (both at work and home).

Research shows there is only one experience in life that increases happiness over the long-term. It's not money, once a base survival threshold is met. It's not marriage, parenthood, or physical health either. The only thing that has been shown to make people happy over the long haul is the *quality and quantity* of their social connections. In fact, a study led by John Cacioppo at the University of Chicago found that loneliness generates a threat response just the same as pain, thirst, fear, or hunger. Consequently, it significantly increases the risk of death from stroke and heart disease.[57]

Pro-Tip: Emotional Deposits

Take two minutes each morning to send a text message or email praising or thanking someone in your life. There are two advantages to this. First, you will have looked over your relationships for something positive to highlight, which will help you see more positives and give more praise. Second, it will make the person on the receiving end feel good, which will make you feel good as well.

Transcend Yourself

We live in a time when most of us have simply lost touch with those who mean the most to us. We're surrounded by surface-level relationships. Who do you turn to when your marriage is on the rocks, or your business is in trouble, or when you're in a state of deep depression or anxiety? Environmentalist Bill McKibben writes, "We've evolved

---

57 Cacioppo, John T., Louise C. Hawkley, and Gary G. Berntson. The Anatomy of Loneliness, *Current Directions in Psychological Science*, June 1, 2003, https://doi.org/10.1111/1467-8721.01232.

into living a neighborless lifestyle; an average American eats half as many meals with family and friends as she did fifty years ago. On average, we have half as many close friends." It's such a paradox, because we're more connected than ever due to the internet, but in many ways people have never felt more alone.

Superficial connections simply don't bring the fulfillment that's required to flourish as humans. Loneliness is painful, and the easiest way to ease the pain is a dopamine spike. And thus, patterns of addiction, pleasure seeking, and hopelessness continue. Viktor Frankl (founder of logotherapy and author of what I consider a must read, *Man's Search for Meaning*) said:

> The meaning of life is to be discovered in the world rather than within man or his own psyche. I have termed this constitutive characteristic the *self-transcendence* of human existence. The more one forgets himself—by giving himself to a cause to serve or another person to love—the more human he is and the more he actualizes himself.

In my own life, I've made serious mistakes and have been in some dark places, from both an emotional and mental perspective. I've found the worst thing I can do in those times is rely on myself. The power of deep-rooted relationships with people you trust in dark times just can't be described. I have a group of four other guys I meet with once a week to discuss personal and spiritual battles, challenges, and successes. I've reached the point where I can tell these guys anything and trust their wisdom, guidance, and accountability with the utmost confidence. Now, it took us about three full years of meeting before we were able to get to that place, but having this outlet has been an invaluable resource, and one I would encourage anyone to begin building. Let me say it very clearly: *You will never become the person you are called to be unless you invest in meaningful, deep, genuine relationships.*

There is very little in life more important than other people. In fact, there may be nothing more important. Your spouse, children, close family, and deepest friendships will bring you the most profound sense of joy and meaning attainable this side of heaven. There are many things in life I'm still learning, but I've found being the father of three daughters teaches me a great deal. Maybe the most important thing I've learned from Kate, Nora, and Lenna is an appreciation for the tenderness of the human heart. I'm the only man in our house with my wife, three daughters, and a female dog. This interesting position has allowed me to observe the *many* weaknesses in my own character and has increased my emotional intelligence a great deal (by necessity).

Not long ago, my middle daughter, Nora, was sick and got an enormous amount of love and attention from both my wife and I while she was getting better. We rubbed her back (even more than normal), we told her how tough and brave she was, and we waited on her hand and foot. Little did I know my oldest daughter, Kate, (our rule-follower) was watching all of this very closely. At bedtime the second night of the ordeal, I noticed Kate had tears in her eyes. I knew what was wrong, but just to confirm, I asked her, "Sweetheart, what's the matter?" She verified my thoughts, saying in the sweetest voice imaginable, "Even though I know Nora is feeling sick, and I asked Jesus to help her get better, I still wish I was getting as much attention as her." She couldn't even be dishonest. She was hungry for emotional connection from her mom and dad, and she couldn't help but say so. I don't blame her a bit. Whether you and I admit it or not, we are all starving for that emotional connection, just like Kate.

Pro-tip: Evaluate Your Current Friendships
Are they deep and authentic, or are they shallow and solely based on fun and distraction? Do your current relationships take you in a direc-

tion not conducive to Shepherd Leadership and Top 1% performance?
Do you have relationships with people who inspire you and make you
want to be better? And finally, do you have friends you really trust and
connect with on a spiritual level? List three things you can do over the
next week to intentionally enhance your existing network of relation-
ships. As you answer these questions, I hope you find that you're in a
great place with deep, meaningful relationships with people you trust.
But if not, don't be discouraged. The opportunity is always there to
take casual relationships and deepen them. Just know you'll likely be
the one who has to take the relationship to the next level.

Your Tribe—the Ultimate Competitive Advantage

The culture you build in your organization and among your team
members is your ultimate competitive advantage. McKinsey and
company have said that "human capital" is the most important asset
in the twenty-first century beyond technology, global positioning,
or operational agility. It will be the most-valued resource over the
next twenty years. An organization becomes the individual people
within it, and the stronger the relationships within the organization,
the stronger the enterprise.

Your number one role as the leader of the tribe is to *lead by example*. Sociologists have determined that human beings learn by mimick-
ing. Your team will see how you behave in given situations, and they
will mimic what you do. When human beings lived nomadic tribal
lifestyles, individuals needed to be accepted by the leader, so they
didn't get left behind. This is innate within us, and the people following your leadership will behave in the same way you do *involuntarily*.
You set the standard, and you set the tone in the organization.

Ray Kroc, founder of McDonalds, said it well: "The quality of
a leader is reflected in the standards they set for themselves." It's as
simple as this: Be the role model you would like to follow.

As a Shepherd Leader, it's crucial for you to leverage your performance to elevate the performance of your organization. One of the most powerful ways to gain leverage is by delegating strategic tasks to trusted members of your team.

Alpha 1.0's often get in trouble here, because (due to a short-term outlook) they refuse to trust members of their team to delegate and gain leverage. The common excuses for this are "It takes too much time" or the classic "I could do it better myself." The problem here is that a lack of proper delegation holds a leader back from going all-in on the highest-leverage activities. It also disempowers the members of your team. They are hungry to be given leadership over their own domains as well. General George S. Patton said: "Never tell people how to do things. Tell them what to do and they will surprise you with their ingenuity."

When you tell people how to do their jobs, you get glorified assistants. But when you *trust and empower* people to get the job done, you create leaders. As a Shepherd Leader, part of your mission is to constantly create other Shepherd Leaders.

But you should delegate in a certain way. The term I prefer to use is empowerment delegation (yes, ED for short; it's easy to remember). With empowerment delegation, the key is to give members of your team autonomy regarding the method or approach they take in performing a given task. The focus here is on results and outcomes, not the ways in which the results are achieved. This gives your team members a lot of responsibility and shows you trust them on a deep level. It turns out that trust is among the highest forms of human motivation.

It takes patience and dedication, but it brings out the very best in all of us. One caveat here is that, as the leader, it's your responsibility (see Behavior #1) to ensure a clear mutual understanding of what a satisfactory result looks like. This is the part that takes an initial bit of patience and time, but in the long run, it's worth it to both you and the members of your team.

Investing in your tribe at work will create the culture that drives the success of your organization. Your role should be conductor of the orchestra, not one of the violinists. You must be in control, but you don't want to be in charge. The ideal is to get the best person possible in each role and then empower them to thrive in their role. As the conductor, you can't play the violin—let the violinists play their own freaking instruments!

Jim Collins said it this way: "Some people, fundamentally, are hard-working and diligent regardless of incentive; it's who they are. Your culture should blow out those who are not." Collins is not referring to some sort of bullying culture. He's saying your team should have such a culture of high-performance and trust that those who are not high-performers won't even feel comfortable working there.

Over the years, I've had people in my organization whom I've loved personally, but the culture was just too much for them. No problem. That's a good thing, because the individuals in the organization must have 100% buy-in for Top 1% organizational performance.

Ten years of data from Gallup found the first 25% of an employee's effort is mandatory, the other 75% is voluntary and based on leadership in culture. Your job is to get that 75%, and you do it through recognition. As Mary Kay Ash said, "The only thing more powerful than sex and money is praise and recognition." Three things people can't give themselves that you must give them are *personal attention*, *appreciation*, and *recognition*. They need to feel valued, they need to feel significance in their work, and they need meaning in their lives. As a Shepherd Leader, you must make it part of your mission to help your team with their lives, not just their jobs.

Value-Producing Assets

The second prong of the Big 3 is recognizing value-producing assets. There are a number of these across your business. They might include things like technology, marketing, and of course people. However, a key misunderstanding most people have (especially Alpha 1.0's) is that they value money over these crucial assets. That has to change, and it can when you better understand that money is simply a currency we use to complete transactions. Money is nothing more than a tool that can be used to create value in opportunity. In and of itself, it has no inherent value. Also understand this: Anyone, including you right now, can create wealth. In fact, 80% of millionaires are first generation millionaires.

The key difference between the poor, the wealthy, and the middle-class, is that the poor buy liabilities like lottery tickets, the wealthy buy assets with true sustainable value, like businesses and real estate, and the middle-class buy liabilities thinking they're buying assets (e.g., real estate that doesn't generate cash).

Assets fall into two separate categories: Hard assets and soft assets. Hard assets are real estate, profitable businesses, and stocks. Soft assets are things like your energy, your education, your time, and your focused attention. It's crucial to invest in each of these, because these are the things that will allow you to create the most value in the world around you.

Pro-Tip: Invest in Developing Expertise

Resolve to become an expert in one of the assets, hard or soft, mentioned here. Expertise has been defined as education plus experience. You will want to begin investing a minimum of 10% of your income on developing expertise. Mentorships, masterminds, and educational experiences in a one-on-one or seminar format are the best investments here. I personally spend between $50,000–$100,000 a year on developing further expertise. You should make the same decision.

The number one asset you have is not money. Rather, it is yourself and your business. The best part is that you have more direct control over those things than any other assets. Your emotional resilience, your tolerance for risk, your ability to create a powerful vision, and your ability to commit to mastery. These are the attributes that have built everything, and these create and generate revenue for you now. No one else did that, that was all you and the team you built.

If you've gotten to this point in the book, and you've not yet begun the process of building your own business, don't panic. It's all good. Remember, Colonel Sanders didn't even start KFC until he was six-ty-six years old, and he did just fine. But I would strongly advise if you have the goal of becoming truly financially abundant, then start your business part-time immediately. Don't waste your time and energy with a part-time job, just keep your full-time employment and begin building a business on the side. The process of becoming a "business owner" is a huge asset in itself.

If you can discipline yourself to build a business, then a whole new world of limitless possibilities will open up for you. In his book *How to be Rich,* J. Paul Getty says his first rule is that you must be in business for yourself. You will never build true wealth working for someone else. The key is to build a business with both a spiritual and financial mission that fills a need for customers by either *adding massive value or removing massive pain.* That is the key. If you can do those things, you will win.

I talk about the importance of my father as a key mentor for me, and this is a lesson I learned from him. The ultimate control over your destiny is when you are in the driver's seat of your business. When you're in that position, the only limiting factor is you and your ability to solve problems.

I will challenge you to stop focusing on ways to pull in money, and start focusing on ways to deliver value. Value is 100% based on the perceptions of your potential customers. Value is produced by delivering convenience and joy, and by alleviating pain, anxiety, and discomfort. Also, value goes deep and is not superficial. A good rule of thumb

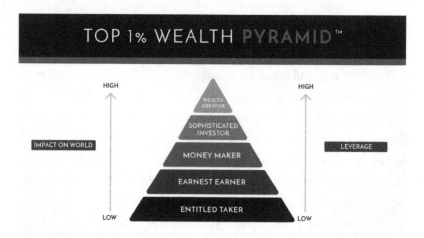

here, which I learned from both Grant Cardone and Eben Pagan, is the concept of 10x value. You must create at least ten times the value you're getting paid for your service or product. This may seem hard to swallow at first, but it's the only way to build serious success.

Look at Building Wealth as a Project

You must view building wealth as a project just like building a relationship, or building a business, or getting into shape. This is a primary characteristic of those who choose the right value-related assets. They know what gets them to the finish line, and they recognize it's not a focus solely on money.

Wake up to the idea you have to choose an area of wealth building that makes sense to you individually (not just something promoted by the mainstream media). Ask yourself if you could spend a decade, or a couple decades, becoming an expert in this area of wealth building to the point where success is inevitable. On a personal level, you really must become fascinated with the idea and process of creating wealth. Just learning about it casually without a deep interest will not allow you to achieve the results you're absolutely desiring to achieve. You must dedicate yourself to it day after day, month after month, and year after year.

It's really important to detach yourself from the material posses-sions involved in building wealth. We're only on this planet for a tem-porary amount of time, so none of the resources are truly ours in the strictest sense. We must serve more as stewards of our resources and use them in a way that's helpful and contributes to the lives of our-selves and others while we're privileged enough to have them. This is an important mindset shift for those who desire to build wealth.

Understanding money is crucial to accumulating wealth. Most people think money actually *is* value. But it's not. Money is not a *cause*, it is an *effect* of creating value. The financially wealthy under-stand this, and they set up systems to create value and accumulate value producing assets. Understand that the majority of your "stuff" falls into the category of liabilities, not assets. The more stuff you own, the less success you can enjoy because you have more stuff to manage. I'm not suggesting you sell everything you own, I'm simply helping you understand the value of assets and the disadvantage of surplus liabilities.

Your Own Education

The final prong of the Big 3 is focusing on your own education. Ralph Waldo Emerson said, "Every man I meet is my master in some point, and in that I learn of him." To become wealthy, the first thing you must do is increase your financial intelligence, or better educate yourself. You must be willing to dedicate the time to learning and seeking out counsel to build long-term wealth. This experience, as well as the edu-cation you acquire along the way, is worth so much more than your actual time investment.

There's a popular story about Pablo Picasso in which he is said to have been drawing on a napkin when he was approached by a woman who asked if she could buy the napkin from him. He told her: "Well, yes, it will be $20,000." She asked why a small drawing on a napkin that only took two minutes of his time would cost $20,000. Picasso responded with a correction: "It didn't take me two minutes. I've been working on that piece of art for sixty years."

There's a pervasive myth that exists in our society known as "overnight success." The media feeds the lie by promoting success story after success story without the reality of the backstory for clarification. The fact is, the thousands of hours of practice, learning, and education, whether formal or self-directed, are never documented unless you dig deep to learn the truth about how the best got to where they are now.

Whether it was an apprenticeship or just dogged determination, all the people you admire most because of their accomplishments have relentlessly invested in their learning and education. I personally spend somewhere between $50,000–$100,000 a year on my own education and learning experiences. These are often in the form of educational events like masterminds and high-performance forums with mentors like Darren Hardy, John Maxwell, Chris Widener, and my mentor in endodontics, Dr. Ace Goerig. Most of these experiences have a combined benefit of building my tribe of business and personal relationships, as well as serving as immense personal growth opportunities.

In my own life, I've found that the more money I invest in something, the more I pay attention. If I haven't put down a financial commitment, then I'm just too casual. And as the great Jim Rohn once said, "Casualness leads to casualties." I bet the same is true in your life. If you haven't invested your money, time, and resources, it's just very difficult to get yourself to go all in. And as I mentioned earlier, you must be COMMITTED (see Behavior #5). The advantage of being a student and a lifelong learner is that it places you in a position of humility and puts the ego on the shelf. To quote Epictetus, "It is impossible to learn that which one thinks one already knows." Learning is inherently egoless.

Benefits of Lifelong Learning

Dedicating yourself to lifelong learning produces a number of benefits. Investments in your own education are an economic necessity. The links between formal education and lifetime earnings have been well-studied. In 2015, Christopher Tamborini, ChangHwan Kim, and Arthur Sakamoto found that, controlling for other factors, men and women can expect to earn $655,000 and $445,000 more, respectively, during their careers with a bachelor's degree than with a high school degree, with graduate degrees yielding even further gains.[58] Outside of universities, ongoing learning and skill development is also essential to surviving economic and technological disruption.

In addition, a series of studies on the benefits of pursuing learning opportunities throughout life found that among other benefits, continued learning leads to an enriching life of self-fulfillment, helps us make new friends and establish valuable relationships, helps us adapt to change, and helps fully develop natural abilities.[59]

So that leads to a very important question: What types of educational investments are best? Well, to begin, I suggest you read consistently. Reading is not only inexpensive and easily accessible, but it's a powerful way to learn. Science confirms that you are what you read. Researchers from both Dartmouth and Ohio State found that when you become deeply invested in a book, you begin to both identify with and take on some of the traits and characteristics of the main character(s).[60] For this reason, focus on books that will build characteristics you want more of in your life. Invest in both physical and audio books. Audio books are great when you're in transit, but there's

---

58 Tamborini, Christopher R. et al. Education and Lifetime Earnings in the United States. *Demography* vol. 52,4, 2015, pp. 1383-407.

59 Nordstrom, N. M. & Merz, J. F. *Learning Later, Living Greater: The Secret for Making the Most of Your After-50 Years*, Boulder, Colorado: Sentient Publications, 2006.

60 See https://hbr.org/2015/09/the-unexpected-influence-of-stories-told-at-work.

no replacement for a physical book you can dog-ear and take notes in. Don't read just for volume of knowledge, but for depth of knowledge. Go deep and re-read books multiple times. Understanding and implementation is the key to real learning. These are your benchmarks. Not quantity, but quality.

Beyond books, podcasts and online courses are phenomenal as well. We now live in a world where online learning is available to nearly anyone, and you must take full advantage of it. Today, books are cheaper than ever, access to teachers is virtually unlimited, and courses are readily available. There is simply no excuse for not getting the education you need, and there is no excuse for ever ending your education. Again, it's quality over quantity. It's easy to get sucked into the trap of buying course after course without adequate implementation of your learning and strategies along the way. I myself have done this many times. The ideal here is to treat any individual online course as a serious investment in your future. Courses can be expensive, but the ROI (return on investment) is nearly always there if you make implementation a priority.

But education and learning doesn't start and stop with mere engagement in media. One of the most powerful ways to learn is to do so from others. That's where the concept of mentorship comes into play. The reason you require a mentor is very simple: Life moves very quickly, and you only have so much time and energy to expend during the greatest years of achievement. In general, the most creative years begin in your late twenties through your late forties. A mentor will speed the process up, so you can buckle down during those crucial years and bring your mission to life. Even in cases where your particular circumstances limit direct contact with the mentor you need, books written by or about these mentors can serve as a substitute, provided you interact deeply with the material, take notes, write in the margins, and connect on a personal level with the mentor's spirit through the writing. In addition, even figures from the past can serve as role models. In my own life, I've studied and connected deeply with figures like John Wooden, Jim Rohn, and the Reverend Billy Graham through their own writings and works written about them.

Another important note about mentorship as it relates to Mastery is that Mastery by nature requires a certain level of suffering, setbacks, and criticism. It's important to have a mentor who will give you a sharp constructive dose of reality. They must be willing to give you the proper challenges that will increase your strengths and give you adequate feedback regardless of how much it may sting your ego. Confidence is crucial, but it must be built on an objective reality of who you *actually* are.

As entrepreneur Michael Fishman said: "Self-made is an illusion. There are many people who played divine roles in you having the life you have today. Be sure to let them know how grateful you are." Remember that it's important to admire and respect your mentors, but your ultimate goal should always be to surpass them in Mastery.

Investing to build wealth should not be overly complicated. If you follow these simple guidelines with commitment and consistency, you can be sure you're putting your most precious resources toward things that will grow in value for you over time. Cultivate your tribe, accumulate value producing assets, and pursue your lifelong quest toward wisdom and understanding. Adopt Behavior #6: Relentlessly Invest in the Big 3.

Exercise: Dropping into the "Zone"

Make a very specific list of ten to fifteen things you're deeply curious about learning. These are things you might spend time reading books about or having conversations about or even spending a weekend diving deeply into. Try not to be vague here but specific. The more specific, the better. For example, don't list something like "sports" or "basketball," but rather "the advantages and disadvantages of matchup zone defense in college basketball."

For example, I'm profoundly interested in spirituality and scientific evidence, as well as success and wealth building. I'm particularly interested in modern advancements in science and technology, quantum physics and string theory, arguments for and against the existence of God, the predictability of learning as it pertains to high-performance and leadership, and things like that.

After you've got your specific list of ten to fifteen things, the next step is to find commonalities and intersections in the list. You're looking for patterns in your list, which your brain loves. It puts you in a state of momentum and increased energy when you find these patterns.

Here's an example from my list: How are the principles of modern science and technology augmenting the evidence for the existence of God? Another is the topic of this particular training program, which is: What does scientific evidence say about the behaviors of super successful leaders and performers, and how can that be turned into a system other people can use to get excellent results? Those are two of mine. Now I want you to make your list. Try to get ten to fifteen if you can, and then find those intersections. Make those connections to build momentum and figure out how you can create a little more flow in your daily life.

Chapter 8

BEHAVIOR #7: BE STILL AND KNOW

Be still, and know that I am God.
~Psalm 46:10~

As a human being, it's in your nature to think: *If I can just make that next sale, or start a new business, or get into that residency program, or get that girl/guy to date me, then I'll be happy.* But thousands of scientific studies have shown this journey to the "next great thing" to be based off false pretense. In fact, the pursuit of happiness is exactly the opposite of this proposed path. The simple act of waiting to be happy actually limits your brain's potential for success. In contrast to this practice, cultivating positivity, peace, and contentment in your brain will increase motivation, productivity, emotional resilience, and your overall performance. Who would think our very idealization and pursuit of something new would actually inhibit our ability to recognize what we might have? It is complicated at best, a non-starter at worst.

Throughout this book I've hinted at an IDEAL with which you must be striving, and a required step of all Shepherd Leaders and Top 1% performers. But in some ways this IDEAL might also leave you with a sense of shame and resentment because you know you'll never get there on your own. And you're right, you can't. But as you've already learned by cultivating Behavior #4, there's much more going on in and around you that isn't immediately apparent. It only becomes truly visible when you take the time to cultivate this final behavior, which I refer to as the concept of Behavior #7: Be Still and Know. Here, we recognize there is an unseen force in eternal existence from which all things originated. You must develop a deep and unshakable faith in that force if you ever plan to move in the direction of your goals. You can call it what you want, but I'll refer to it as God.

The term "faith," as I use it here, is not some naïve belief in magic or a higher spirit. It's the willingness to strive for the seemingly impossible task of reaching the IDEAL and trusting that on a spiritual (dare I say supernatural) level, there is a real Force conspiring on your behalf to help elevate and empower you toward your goals and dreams. This type of faith requires *all of you*. It requires sacrifice, self-discipline, and immense courage. It also requires that you place the first six behaviors in motion in your life. Even so, this behavior is like gas on a fire. It will make every other behavior easier and more powerful for you. Ultimately, it's about "religion" as we've come to understand it in the modern sense. No one in history was more critical of religion than Christ. In fact, if you read the gospels, Jesus always condemned the high-brows in positions of religious authority. And ultimately that's why he was killed. So set aside any assumptions that Behavior #7 is somehow untouchable to those who don't believe in Jesus, God, or any higher spirit. You too have access to this.

In his 1978 commencement address at Harvard, Aleksandr Solzhenitsyn described the modern crisis of human "despiritualization" in the following remarks:[61]

> Man is the touchstone in judging everything on earth—imperfect man, who is never free of pride, self-interest, envy, vanity, and dozens of other defects . . . On the way from the Renaissance to our days we have enriched our experience, but we have lost the concept of a *supreme complete entity* which used to restrain our passions and our irresponsibility. We placed too much hope in political and social reforms, only to find out that we were being deprived of our most precious possession: *our spiritual life* (Emphasis mine).

Always remember: You are a spiritual being, living in a physical body, and gifted with a mind. Your spiritual component is really who *you* are, so you must not neglect it. Have you ever taken the time to just sit and enjoy the idea that you exist? To take things even farther, have you ever pondered that anything at all exists? If you haven't done so lately, I recommend you do so now. The sense of calm and inner peace that comes from the simple act of reflection and gratitude for all that is, all that was, and all that will be isn't comparable with anything else you'll experience. You shouldn't exist at all, yet you do. Just think about that and let it bring a smile of contentment to you right now.

After adopting Behavior #4: Strategically Design Your Reality, is it such a stretch to accept something bigger and beyond you that isn't apparent by immediate observation? Obviously not. Notable (and perhaps surprising) Top 1% performers of deep faith include people like

---

61 See https://www.americanrhetoric.com/speeches/alexandersolzhenitsynharvard.htm.

Stephen Colbert, Mark Wahlberg, Denzel Washington, Tony Dungy, Tom Hanks, Dr. Ben Carson, Muhammad Ali, and Kanye West. Each of these remarkable human beings have found a way to incorporate deep faith into their very existence and daily activities. In doing so, they have found connection and meaningful direction in all they are and all they do.

As Jordan Peterson describes, in Genesis 1, God creates the world with divine order from the previous swirling chaos. He even pronounces the creation as "good" at each step of the process. Unfortunately, as the story unfolds, we find that the Fall, the Great Flood, and the Tower of Babel each destroy that initial order and "goodness." But each of us remembers in some way what things were once like, and we long for that IDEAL once again. We maintain nostalgia for the innocence and magic of childhood, but more than that, we have what might be called a God-shaped void in our hearts that can only be filled by the divine. This is even present in the staunchest atheist who experiences the peace associated with the beauty and awe of nature and the cosmos. You somehow know there's something greater, and you need connection with it.

There is a war raging inside you. If not properly managed, the war inside you will make its way outside of you and create violence and destruction in the external world. Anxiety, depression, posttraumatic stress disorder, and senseless violence are at epidemic levels. The only way to solve this is by cultivating an inner peace that can only be found through deep spiritual connection with a higher power.

You cannot fulfill your purpose if you're focused on approval, applause, and affirmation from the world around you. It may not come, and even if it does, it won't satisfy your soul. However, if you live for the glory of God, you stop looking for approval and affirmation from others, and instead start throwing yourself into your calling without self-obsession. You find contentment in knowing you're fulfilling your purpose and Major Mastery Mission, and this glorifies your Creator. You may recall the classic line from *Chariots of Fire* when Scottish Olympian and missionary Eric Liddell says: "I believe God made me for a purpose, but he also made me fast. And when I run I feel His pleasure." Take the time now to ask yourself, "How can I feel His pleasure?" Or if you prefer, "How can I connect with my calling in such a way that I feel a deep sense of spiritual connection?"

As a committed Shepherd Leader, you may feel as if you're in a bit of a dilemma. You are responsible for more than any single person is equipped to handle, yet you must handle it with grace and thoughtful direction. You're meant to carry a burden and responsibility that very well may lead to burn-out and hopelessness if you don't cultivate the inner strength that comes only from deep spiritual connection. As much as you might try, you will not be able to do what is demanded of you without resources and energy *beyond your own.*

You also need wisdom that's beyond your own capability as you help others navigate life. You will need to ask God for wisdom and understanding throughout each and every day to be at your best. All of creation is designed to be at its optimal when in concert with God's supernatural will and provision. Human beings in general, and you specifically, are no exception to this rule. You simply can't live up to God's standards without first embracing God's resources.

Your Belief Is the Key

Science is important, knowledge must be sought after, and diligent strategy and pragmatic planning are essential pieces of the Shepherd Leadership puzzle. But you must *believe* in something. You must believe in an eternal purpose that you're designed to fulfill. Look at your challenges, your suffering, and your interactions with others in light of *eternity*. If you're going to be a legendary leader and hero to yourself and others, you simply have no alternative. One of my all-time favorite thinkers, C.S. Lewis, summed the idea up so beautifully when he said the following:

> There are no *ordinary* people. You have never talked to a mere mortal. Nations, cultures, arts, civilizations—these are mortal, and their life is to ours as the life of a gnat. But it is immortals whom we joke with, work with, marry, snub and exploit . . . .[62]

As we were driving home one evening, my middle daughter, Nora, asked me a profound question. As she looked out the window, she asked, "Daddy, what moon do they see in Paris?"

The question brought tears to my eyes, both because of its pure innocence and because of the ah-ha moment it provided for me (I'm a little slow, okay). In that moment, I was overwhelmed by the realization that the moon Nora and I were enamored with at that instant was not only the very same moon that everyone living in the world now sees, but also the same moon experienced by every human being who has ever lived!

But here's the big takeaway from that profound question from my supremely observant little girl: You and I, and every human being who has ever lived, are much more alike than we are different. We are all unique, but we are also deeply connected by the warm radiating feeling that only comes when you experience true and pure love. Jesus Christ felt this, but so did Hitler. The objects of their love were vastly different, but the essential feeling was common to each of them in the depths of their souls, just as it is to me and you.

In equal measure, we are linked by our common understanding and sensation of deep pain. The despair associated with the loss of a loved one, the stress of having too much month at the end of the money, the bitterness of divorce, the guilt after an indiscretion. These universal sensations connect us as well. We're all in this thing called life together. Remember, we really are all on the same team.

---

62   See http://www.wheelersburg.net/Downloads/Lewis%20Glory.pdf.

C.S. Lewis was right. Indeed, there are no mere mortals (yourself included). Think of this in every meaningless dispute with your spouse, every time you discipline your child, each time you are tempted to let anger get the best of you, and, yes, even when another immortal cuts you off in traffic and flips you the bird. You're a Shepherd Leader now. No excuses.

Mark Twain said: "The fear of death follows from the fear of life. A man who lives fully is prepared to die at any time." Fear sucks away all your energy, but deep faith energizes. You must integrate faith-building practices and behaviors.

Coming to grips with the reality of your own mortality is crucial because it cuts through all the superficial crap you tend to prioritize in your brief time on earth. Sure, money is important, but it's only a tool for making an impact. In and of themselves, money, fame, and power are only tools for accomplishing the real things in life that are important. The real questions that matter include: How will the world be different and better because of you? What positive influence will you have had on those you encounter? What impact will you have made? The certainty of death must be the centerpiece around which we organize all our other choices and values. The only way to become comfortable with this idea is by having faith in and connecting with something far beyond yourself.

This posture is the opposite of entitlement. The entitled person is the center of all the unfairness and challenges in the universe. His/her attention is inward and self-focused. This position inherently forfeits all responsibility and mandates that society at large take care of everything for them. This entitled group feels deserving of something without earning it and feels the right to everything without having sacrificed to make it happen. This attitude will poison your soul and destroy the possibility for true fulfillment and meaningful contribution. It simply doesn't allow for the peace of mind that comes when you're able to "be still and know."

The War in the Human Heart

The real war that's ultimately responsible for all other wars is the one in the human heart. It's the war within. Each of us battles envy, pride, bitterness, guilt, and discontentment. These battles make up the pieces of war. And one thing we know is what happens inside your heart deeply impacts what happens in your external world. As Jesus himself put it: "What good will it be for someone to gain the whole world, yet forfeit their soul?"

We each desperately need peace, but it often seems elusive to us human beings. In the Bible, in the book of Job specifically, Job suffers greatly. He says, "What I feared has come upon me; what I dreaded has happened to me. I have no peace, no quietness; I have no rest, but only turmoil."

If you're honest with yourself, you've probably felt this way at some point in your life. You might even feel that way now. Worry robs you of joy, and fear robs you of freedom. It robs you of the strength, confidence, and courage it takes to succeed at the highest level. The life you're meant to live is one of strength and courage as a Top 1% performer.

Paradoxically, stillness, faith, and peace don't come when you have control over every aspect of your life. Deep peace and faith are only cultivated when you relinquish the need for total control. The previous six behaviors are behaviors I urge you to work on and build into your life. But Behavior #7 is equally critical and involves your deepest understanding that many things are not within your control. That's okay, though. It's more than okay. It's the way life was designed to be. Accepting it, embracing it, and building a deeper spiritual connection with your Creator (who does have ultimate control) is critical.

Absolutely take control of the things you can, but relinquish control of the things you cannot. It's only by creating deep peace within yourself that you can introduce peace to the world around you. This inner stillness I'm talking about doesn't come from having learned enough, or from knowing everything, but instead comes from knowing and accepting that *learning will never cease*. It's a deep wisdom that comes only from spiritual connection.

Wisdom Is Strength

To "be still and know" is the process of cultivating wisdom. And wisdom is strength. Wisdom is knowing you'll never know it all, and that you must rely on God's guidance throughout the journey. Even at the very highest level of performance there will be times where you feel limited and unable to deal with certain challenges or overcome certain obstacles. It's during these times that you must lean on a higher power.

As a Shepherd Leader and Top 1% performer, it's your responsibility to make time for deep thought and critical analysis. As I've alluded to earlier, you have access to more information than you could ever reasonably need. This can overwhelm the mind. It's important that you refuse the habit of following current events minute-by-minute, and instead focus on a few important performance indicators in your personal, spiritual, and professional life. Don't allow the fear of missing out to pull your attention away from the game-changing habits and activities. Epictetus said, "If you wish to improve, be content to appear clueless or stupid in extraneous matters."

It's a waste of time and energy to consume the news in real time, and it's only your primal self that desires to be the most informed and updated person in the room. And for God's sake, refuse to let your inbox rule your life! If you allow yourself to check your inbox throughout the day without any structure or systematic approach, you'll become a slave to the agendas of those (often well-meaning) people and businesses sending you emails. A healthier and much more focused way to deal with your inbox is to designate two to three well-defined blocks of time solely devoted to managing emails. Using this approach will allow your mind the freedom to focus on your work, family, and other important pursuits without the nagging desire to check emails. This will help you conserve valuable mental energy and ease your mind.

Relaxation, focus, and presence are three states of consciousness that are very uncommon in our present time. If you're busy it's very hard to be present. And unless you're present, nothing powerful can take place. Busyness kills your ability to be present.

The great general and leader President Dwight D. Eisenhower found himself overwhelmed by the amount of information coming at him in his role as commander-in-chief. Knowing this state of mind wasn't conducive to high-performance, he came up with what is now known as the Eisenhower Matrix.[63] Eisenhower found most things were urgent but not important. However, the important things were not necessarily time sensitive. So he made it a policy for his staff to review all incoming information and categorize it as either urgent or important. He would most likely delegate those issues that were urgent and spend his mental energy on the important tasks that required his highest level of thinking.

Wisdom is strength, and this comes from not just understanding what you do know, but also recognizing that you might not know everything. Accepting that is an important step toward finding peace. As you begin this process of acceptance, you can then filter information that's readily available to you. Wisdom is not just listening, but also ignoring stimuli that are not particularly positive or helpful to your growth.

Pro-Tip: Designated Gatekeeper

Designate a person on your team to be the gatekeeper between you and the outside world. You must conserve your mental energy for big

---

63   See https://www.eisenhower.me/eisenhower-matrix.

picture important thinking, strategy, and execution. The gatekeeper is not to allow any drop-in visitors, random or unorganized pieces of information, or emails that have not been properly vetted prior to reaching you. This will be your version of the Eisenhower Matrix. In addition, you can empower members of your team to handle all urgent matters that are not important. This will free you up to work on those important projects and decisions that really move the needle for you, your team, and your business.

I'm going to suggest you adopt another practice in your life. Keep a notebook or journal of some type to record your daily insights, and review the positives and negatives experienced throughout the day. The list of those who stood by their practice of journaling includes Marcus Aurelius, Ralph Waldo Emerson, Benjamin Franklin, John Quincy Adams, Seneca, and Leonardo da Vinci. In fact, da Vinci physically kept his notebooks with him at all times to record his thinking and any new information he found worth noting. We now have research showing that journaling helps improve emotional well-being after stress and trauma, and that those recovering from divorce are better able to recover and move forward positively by incorporating journaling into their daily routine.[64]

There's no right or wrong way to begin journaling. I personally journal on the Google Docs app on my phone during the day to jot down notes quickly, and I have multiple notebooks at home for physical writing as well. Journaling at night is especially beneficial, as it allows you to reflect on the day and make notes and observations. Journal the way that works best for you. The only key thing is to do it consistently.

---

64   Baikie, K. A., & Wilhelm, K. (2005). Emotional and physical health benefits of expressive writing. *Advances in Psychiatric Treatment, 11*, 338-346. doi:10.1192/apt.11.5.338

The Primal Self

Remember, you don't have to pretend to be something you're not, because what you are is already infinitely powerful. There's a divine axis that exists between the center of you and the higher power that exists deep in your soul. This is your spiritual connection with the "uncaused first cause" of the universe that keeps everything moving.

Since becoming a father, I've learned how close children are to the divine Creator. They haven't lived long enough to have lost that connection. The purity and divine nature of children is almost overwhelming the more you observe them.

Unfortunately, adulthood brings scars, insecurities, and impurities that create a perception of distance between us and the divine. It may be that the greatest sin of our time is superficiality. We just don't treasure the spiritual things, the unseen realm, like we should. If we're honest, we just don't feel worthy of divine things. But if you would simply be still, you would understand you were created by something divine, and that you can have connection with that Creator, because the Creator deeply desires connection with you. But it requires that you "be still and know" to get to that place. That is where the primal self takes over.

The primal self is always trying to reinvent itself. This is called personal development. It's not inherently bad, and I believe in it, but it's incomplete. You need to access the higher power that's already within you. This is what it means to "be still and know." Cultivate a faith so deep and intense in something beyond yourself that it's unshakeable. This often happens when you reach (and acknowledge) a situation that is beyond your ability to handle. You cannot forgive, you cannot control your anger. Your lust for money, or power, or sex dictates your choices and you can't stop it.

Perfect. Now you're broken down just enough to take the process of cultivating an unshakeable faith seriously. When you find yourself in a pit so deep that it seems like there's no way out (and you will), it'll be the waking up of your divine higher self that will make all the difference (see Behavior #2). Let's discuss how we can unlock this remarkable potential.

How to Be Still

You may or may not be familiar with the term *mindfulness*. Studies show measurable benefits related to the practice of mindfulness meditation, even in just a few minutes a day. Researchers are finding increases in gray matter in the prefrontal cortex of the brain, which as we discussed earlier is where decision making, logical reasoning, and planning takes place. It's the part of your brain that makes you human.

The prefrontal cortex is also very important in transitioning out of stress and into recovery and rest. Using mindfulness meditation to strengthen the prefrontal cortex allows you to observe stress and respond to it more objectively, almost as a neutral observer, then actively *choose* what to do next.

In contrast, a prefrontal cortex that is weak is easily overwhelmed by stressful situations (see Behavior #2). Mindfulness meditation is a predictable way to tap into your higher self and optimize it by strengthening this mindfulness muscle. There are many ways to do this, but here's one example of how you can be still:

1. Choose a time with minimal distractions (first thing in the morning or just before bed).
2. Sit upright in a quiet space, in a comfortable position.
3. Set a timer (to eliminate the tendency to focus on the passage of time).
4. Breathe deeply in and out through your nose using the Quadrant Breathing technique.
5. Focus exclusively on the sensation of breathing, and if thoughts arise just notice them and let them pass.
6. Begin with one minute and add thirty seconds every few days.

Note: Frequency is more important than the duration of each session. Daily meditation is the ideal, even if that means keeping each session short.

Studies show that just seven to ten minutes of meditation enhance both physiological recovery as well as creativity.[65] In fact, just as we discussed purpose in life (PIL) almost being a magic pill regarding its physiological benefits, meditation is very similar. The other documented benefits of meditation include increased energy, increased willpower, improved sleep, and a more disciplined diet.[66]

Renewal Is Required

I've noticed an underlying shame associated with resting among highly driven individuals. As author Stephen King puts it, "For me, not working is the real work." I must confess this is also a huge challenge for me. I'm so driven that even on vacation I find it challenging to unplug. In fact, on the first vacation my wife and I went on after getting married, I brought several textbooks for my residency program so I could work ahead. I recognize now how that's a pathological approach, but at the time it seemed logical to me. Thankfully, my wife "gets" me (God bless her), and she was patient with some of my more bizarre tendencies. But try to understand how feeling guilty for not working is a detrimental view that will hinder your performance.

65 Brain, Behavior, and Immunity; Volume 27, January 2013, Pages 174-184; A comparison of mindfulness-based stress reduction and an active control in modulation of neurogenic inflammation

66 La Cour and Peterson, "Effects of Mindfulness Meditation on Chronic Pain," *Pain Medicine*, 16(4), 2015, pp. 641-52; Y.Y. Tang, M.I. Posner, M.K. Rothbart, and N.D. Volkow, "Circuitry of Self-Control and It's Role in Reducing Addiction," *Trends in Cognitive Sciences*, 19(4), 2015, pp. 439-444; J.C. Ong, R. Manber, Z. Segal, Y. Zia, S. Shapiro, and J.K. Wyatt. "A Randomized Controlled Trial of Mindfulness Meditation for Chronic Insomnia," *Sleep*, 37(9), 2014, pp. 1553-63; S.N. Ketterman, B.M. Kleinman, M.M. Hood, L.M. Nackers, and J.A. Corsica, "Mindfulness meditation as an Intervention for Binge Eating, Emotional Eating, and Weight Loss: A Systematic Review," *Eating Behaviors*, 15(2), 2014, pp. 197-204.

The fact is, if you never build in meaningful rest periods, then you'll never be able to go full throttle during the intense periods of stress that are required for exponential growth. The concept of a weekend as we know it today was devised in the early 1900s to allow both the Christian and Jewish Sabbath days of rest. However, very few of us actually observe these days of rest as they were originally contemplated.

Instead, we use our weekends to catch up on work or add additional stress from other areas of our lives into those sacred days. This comes at a high cost because it decreases your growth and the quality of the work you do during the week. Studies show how vigor and performance increase following a day of rest. The more someone rests on the weekend, the more productive they are during the week. Also, regarding longer periods of rest like vacations, research shows that breaks lasting seven to ten days have positive effects on health, emotions, and motivation that can last up to thirty days. There's even literature on how a weeklong vacation can eliminate the signs of burnout. To that end, we can look at the exponential growth formula to offer us a clear pathway to healthy renewal:

Intense Stress + Intentional Rest = Exponential Growth

Pro-Tip: Intentional Time Off

1. *Regardless of your type of work, commit to taking at least one and possibly two complete days off every week.*
2. *On both days off and during extended vacations, I want you to truly disconnect from your work. This means you need to unplug physically, mentally, and emotionally. Only engage in activities that bring you relaxation and recovery.*

We control the stress we allow into our lives. But we balk at dedicating time to rest and recharge. Far too often we put intentional rest very low on our list of priorities. That shouldn't be the case. It's as crucial to your success as your education, knowledge, and experience.

Sleep for Success

According to the National Sleep Foundation, 65% of Americans get less than the recommended seven to nine hours of sleep each night. You somehow think you're missing out on something when you're sleeping, but you're actually putting yourself in a position of vulnerability by sleeping less than the optimal amount. Physiologically, sleep is one of the most productive things you can do.

A preeminent sleep researcher at Harvard, Dr. Robert Stickgold,[67] has proven that we process experiences and integrate information gathered while we're awake during sleep at a very deep level. Since Stickgold's foundational research in 2000, many other studies have confirmed the results. In addition to integration of knowledge as well as creativity, researchers at Clemson University have done a series of studies confirming the importance of adequate sleep on your self-control. Specifically, they found that people who don't get enough sleep perform worse on anything that requires focused attention and effort, whether it be learning skills, solving challenging problems, or sticking to a new diet or workout regimen.

Most sleep loss is related to the devices we all use. Researchers at Harvard studied the effects of blue light, which is emitted from all digital devices with screens, whether they be computers, televisions, iPads, or smartphones. They had participants read from either a traditional book or an e-book before going to bed. After five days of this, they found that those reading the e-book reported feeling far less tired when it was time to go to sleep. Physiologically, the e-book readers that were exposed to the blue light experienced a ninety-minute delay in the release of melatonin—the hormone that makes you feel sleepy. Their circadian rhythms had shifted, making it harder for them to fall asleep and feel rested when waking up.

---

67   See https://sleep.med.harvard.edu/people/faculty/220/Robert+Stickgold+PhD.

It's so important to literally be still to get adequate rest. Your Major Mastery Mission and the meaningful goals you'll accomplish along the way to the Top 1% require the most optimized version of you. Rest, renewal, and deep spiritual connection are requirements for you as a Shepherd Leader and Top 1% performer. Adopt Behavior #7: Be Still and Know.

Chapter 9

GOING ALL IN

This is the true joy in life, being used for a purpose
recognized by yourself as a mighty one; being thoroughly
worn out before you are thrown on the scrap heap; being
a force of nature instead of a feverish, selfish little clod of
ailments and grievances complaining that the world will not
devote itself to making you happy.
~George Bernard Shaw~

S o far in this book, you've learned about a systematic set of consistent behaviors that, if practiced regularly, will bring you two powerful skillsets:

1. Mastery of Self

2. Authentic Leadership

As you can imagine, these intersect and substantially relate to one another. For example, as you master your own personal inhibitions and behaviors, you can then authentically lead others by transforming into a person they trust for guidance, protection, and security. The result is that your personal work illuminates the lives of others, and you become an asset to your family, friends, and community. The fruits are worth the labor, but not everyone is willing to put in the work to get to this wonderful finish line.

It's at this point in our journey together that you have a decision to make.

Are you all in?

Are you willing to not just learn, but implement what you've learned to make miraculous things happen in your life and the lives of those you lead?

It's time to make that decision for yourself, because it's human instinct to mimic the actions of our leaders. Remember—when your employees see you behaving a certain way, they'll take on that behavior. So if you want your team to be the best it can be, then you must be the best YOU can be. Remember what Mark Twain said: "Do the right thing. It will gratify some people and astonish the rest." Take the time, energy, and introspection to be the role model you'd want to follow. Doing so can unlock doors that might otherwise remain closed to you and those around you.

How do you envision your future self?

Will you look and act the same as you do now?

After reading this book, I certainly hope that won't be the case. I hope you envision the next version of you, the more evolved version, the more open and empathetic and supportive version, the more confident version, the version that guides even more gracefully than you do today—no matter how incredible you already are. It all begins with your vision and what you can imagine for yourself. Don't be afraid to imagine big. Bruce Lee once said, "To me, the function and duty of a quality human being is the sincere and honest development of one's potential."

It seems to be an innate God-given characteristic to crave greatness. Who doesn't want to be the best at their job? Or a great mentor? A remarkable leader? Much of the depression in our world today is likely caused by a generalized inability to reach our own potential. I believe every human being has a deep-down desire to be great. As we look at this in terms of the Four Levels of Personal Performance, remember: We all crave Mastery; no one desires Mediocrity. But the problem is we don't know what Mastery looks like. We don't have a picture in our mind's eye of the ideal Shepherd Leader. My sincerest intention is that the behaviors outlined in this book inspire you to be an artist and paint your own picture of *how* you're called to behave and *who* you must be to reach the Top 1%.

I have an immense amount of respect for the legendary Jay Abraham. Recently, I had the opportunity to meet Jay in a roundtable discussion. I was fortunate enough to have him as a guest on our *Redefining the Top 1%* podcast. Jay has spent the last forty years working in over a thousand different industries as a business growth strategist and consultant. He is revered by people like Tony Robbins, Brian Tracy, Daymond John, and Fran Tarkenton.

While I was interested in learning business ideas and strategies from Jay, I was particularly interested in his theories on leadership. After all, he's done nothing but solve challenging problems for a living at the highest level for the last four decades. It ended up being a fascinating conversation, and there were a few ideas I found very powerful. One thing he said resonated with me: "People are silently begging to be led—but only by someone they trust who has their best interests in mind."

He also emphasized the fact that every human being (regardless of success level) needs guidance to improve and progress. But perhaps the greatest insight I received from Jay was this: "Business leaders often hire people to help themselves on their crusade of building a bigger, better business; but what they don't realize is that every individual on the team has their own unique set of hopes, challenges, dreams, and problems. And by *choosing* to work with you in your business, they're tying themselves to your wagon and putting their faith in your guidance and protection." Without either of us realizing it, he had solidified the idea of Shepherd Leadership with this one thoughtful insight. As leaders, we must recognize the duty we have to bring a sense of security to those we lead.

My primary recommendation for you is to commit to consistency and accountability as you work to build these behaviors into your daily life. Small yet steady steps of each behavior have the potential to create compounding results. It's not about overnight success. The myth of overnight success is just that—a myth. In fact, the legendary comedian Steve Martin addressed this idea of success when he said, "I did stand-up comedy for eighteen years—ten of those years were spent learning, four years were spent refining, and four years were spent in wild success. The course was more plodding than heroic."

While my intention for you is to reach significant levels of success by implementing these behaviors within months (not years), like Steve's, your journey won't feel heroic most of the time. That's just the process. I recommend you not only utilize the exercises outlined in this book, but that you take advantage of the expansive *Redefining the Top 1%* PDF workbook. This workbook has an expansive list of practical exercises and routines to take your commitment to Shepherd Leadership to the next level.

My last piece of advice is to take on this challenge with another current or aspiring leader. You'll need someone you can check in with, be honest and vulnerable with, and whom you can trust to hold you accountable. This person can serve as a thinking partner, a study partner, and someone to help you keep your commitments. If you're looking for a community of people who are already studying and implementing these behaviors in their lives, I invite you to join our free Redefining the Top 1% Facebook community.

And finally, if you want the most efficient program for building Shepherd Leadership, I created our flagship program, The Personal Leadership Academy, specifically for you. Each of these resources offers additional prospects for you to supplement your personal and professional life, and to work on the leadership qualities outlined in this book. Please review these and use them to continue your learning.

I'd like to share two final points of emphasis with you. The first is that you should always remember this journey is uniquely your own. As Theodore Roosevelt pointed out, "Comparison is the thief of joy." If you want to impact others, reach the top, and experience true joy, you must stop comparing. Far too often, you and I look at other people and make their approval the standard we feel obligated to meet. As a consequence, we waste our own unique potential and never pursue our individual missions for mastery. Instead, choose leadership by determining the path of your life.

To invoke the words of another historic leader, Viktor Frankl, "Everyone has his own specific vocation or mission in life . . . Therein he cannot be replaced, nor can his life be repeated. Thus, everyone's task is as unique as his specific opportunity to implement it." Do not compare your mission to that of others. Just strive to fulfill yours to the best of your ability. The rest will take care of itself. Life isn't ultimately about you. Shepherd Leaders not only recognize this, but act in concert with it. Sadly, most leaders never learn this lesson. It's difficult to swallow at first, but I've found the more I focus on propping myself up, the more miserable I feel, and the more inadequate I'm shown to be.

There's a certain personality type that never really wants to be happy, they just want to talk about being happy in the future. Call it Type A, call it Alpha, call it whatever you want. In my case, I'd call it me for the majority of my thirty-seven years. There's nothing wrong with never settling. But the danger in building your life around future goals is that you're constantly striving. If you're addicted to striving, there's little room to invest in those you're present with right now.

Dr. Wayne Dyer called this the disease of more. The challenge is that even when we reach the goals we've been striving for, the moment we arrive we don't know what to do because we've been addicted to striving for so long. This causes further discontentment, because we are so addicted to striving. Dyer called the present moment the "working unit" of life.

Don't ever forget life is meant to be a series of challenges that can turn us into who we were designed to be. The best version of you is the one in which you're helping others by guiding, supporting, and protecting them. That's where true joy, peace, and fulfillment in life is found. You can make this happen now. Life gets so much better when you put "we" above "I." Build up your team, not just yourself.

My deepest hope is that this book helped you shift your paradigm to recognize just how impactful you can be. In each of us lies a great deal of potential to rise above and inspire greatness. As you read these parting words, I'm confident you should be moved to action. To begin analyzing your behaviors, and work to change those you feel do not fully serve you. Do that, and you will feel a remarkable shift. Success and fulfillment is then within reach.

Thank you for your time and dedication in reading this book. It has been a labor of love, my life's purpose. I sincerely wish you and those you lead the best success imaginable as you create your own path to the Top 1%.

With love and support,

Trevor

ABOUT THE AUTHOR

D r. Trevor Blattner is a Business Performance Coach, the Host of *Redefining The Top 1%*, and leading thinker on Shepherd Leadership -- a modern approach to leadership designed to address a world that is complex and ever-changing.

With over 20 years of research, coaching, and experience, Trevor has developed a model of leadership that breaks free of antiquated and regressive notions of what it means to lead. His enlightened approach to leadership is based on behavioral science, personal experience, and a strong commitment to personal values.

The founder of a seven figure business, Trevor is no stranger to adversity and is used to working with people of all backgrounds. He has experienced first-hand that the road to your top 1% is not without challenges. It's through this lens that he's now committed himself to helping individuals overcome their setbacks, eliminate self-doubt and perform without limits in business and life.

As the host of *Redefining The Top 1%,* he's interviewed guests ranging from New York Times Best-selling authors to global influencers to executives of multi-billion-dollar companies – all designed to understand their keys to breaking through.

Trevor has been featured in Conscious Millionaire, Addicted to Success, The Good Men Project, Empowered Living, and Podcast Magazine among others.

In addition to his business success, Trevor is the proud father of three beautiful girls and is married to an amazing wife, Ashley who has been the backbone to his journey. Trevor can be contacted directly at TB@drtrevorblattner.com

A free ebook edition
is available with the
purchase of this book.

To claim your free ebook edition:

1. Visit MorganJamesBOGO.com
2. Sign your name CLEARLY in the space
3. Complete the form and submit a photo of the entire copyright page
4. You or your friend can download the ebook to your preferred device

Morgan James BOGO™

A **FREE** ebook edition is available for you or a friend with the purchase of this print book.

CLEARLY SIGN YOUR NAME ABOVE

Instructions to claim your free ebook edition:
1. Visit MorganJamesBOGO.com
2. Sign your name CLEARLY in the space above
3. Complete the form and submit a photo of this entire page
4. You or your friend can download the ebook to your preferred device

Print & Digital Together Forever.

Snap a photo

Free ebook

Read anywhere

9 781631 953262